THE OLD TESTAMENT

THE OLD TESTAMENT

A Brief Introduction

CHRISTOPH LEVIN

TRANSLATED BY
MARGARET KOHL

PRINCETON UNIVERSITY PRESS

PRINCETON AND OXFORD

Copyright © 2005 by Princeton University Press
Published by Princeton University Press, 41 William Street, Princeton,
New Jersey 08540
In the United Kingdom: Princeton University Press, 3 Market Place,
Woodstock, Oxfordshire OX20 1SY
All Rights Reserved

Originally published in German as *Das Alte Testament*, copyright © 2001
by Verlag C. H. Beck oHG, Munich
ISBN: 0-691-11394-7
Library of Congress Cataloging-in-Publication Data
Levin, Christoph, 1950–
[Alte Testament. English.]
The Old testament: a brief introduction / Christoph Levin; translated by
Margaret Kohl.
p. cm.
Includes bibliographical references.
ISBN 0-691-11394-7 (cl: alk. paper)
1. Bible. O.T.—Commentaries. I. Title.
BS1151.52.L48 2005
221.6'1—dc22
2004058693

British Library Cataloging-in-Publication Data is available
This book has been composed in Palatino with
Copperplate Gothic Light display
Printed on acid-free paper. ∞
www.pup.princeton.edu
Printed in the United States of America
1 3 5 7 9 10 8 6 4 2

CONTENTS

CONTENTS

CONTENTS

CONTENTS

CONTENTS

LIST OF ABBREVIATIONS

Complete bibliographical information is available in the section entitled Further Reading, under Anthologies of Ancient Near Eastern Texts in English Translation (page 189f.).

AEL   *Ancient Egyptian Literature: A Book of Readings, I–III* (Lichtheim)

AHI   *Ancient Hebrew Inscriptions: Corpus and Concordance* (Davies)

ANET   *Ancient Near Eastern Texts Relating to the Old Testament*, 3d ed. (Pritchard)

BWL   *Babylonian Wisdom Literature* (Lambert)

COS   *The Context of Scripture* (Hallo and Younger)

TUAT   *Texte aus der Umwelt des Alten Testaments* (Kaiser)

THE OLD TESTAMENT

WHY READ THE OLD TESTAMENT?

Like all the great things which humanity has created in the course of its history, the Old Testament has a power which immediately communicates itself to everyone who encounters it with open eyes and ears. With immense force, it puts forward its own understanding of what it is, and outruns every attempt at interpretation. But this in itself makes us curious. How can a work like this have come into being? The question is particularly insistent because, although it has its source in the Ancient Near East, this book has influenced the religion and culture of the West like no other.

At present, Old Testament scholarship is in the process of striking out in a new direction, and this again makes it a particularly exciting discipline within the field of historical studies. It is becoming increasingly clear that ancient Hebrew literature has to be read as a part of Ancient Near Eastern culture and religion. The comparable texts from ancient Mesopotamia and Egypt, the Hittite empire and Ugarit have, many of them, been known for a long time; but they are being increasingly opened up, and are appearing in a new light. The literary genres and themes we find in the

Old Testament, its social background—even ancient Israel's concept of God—are no longer without analogy. Sensational inscription discoveries are shedding light on the "subliterary" "folk" religion of Israel and Judah. Iconographic interpretation in particular is contributing to a new view, since it allows Old Testament texts to speak with surprising eloquence through the medium of Ancient New Eastern picture symbolism. The archaeology of Palestine—above all investigation into the early settlement—is also teaching us to understand the social environment better.

On the other hand, analytical exegesis, especially as it is treated in German-language research, is penetrating ever more deeply into the Old Testament text, and shows that its emergence is for the most part the outcome of a long process of literary self-interpretation, the presuppositions for which can no longer be looked for in the monarchies of Israel and Judah, but actually belong to the postexilic Judaism of the Second Temple period. For this branch of biblical research, to a far greater extent than has hitherto been accepted, the Old Testament can no longer be seen as the literature of ancient Israel, but is in its very roots the Holy Scripture of the Judaism of the Persian and Hellenistic periods.

For the history of religion, the Old Testament is significant because it marks the threshold between a Palestinian national cultic religion and what has been called "ethical monotheism." With the Old Testament, religion begins to ask about its universally valid truth, and arrives at a radically transcendent view of God, in which religion is inextricably bound up with ethics, and love of God (Deut. 6:4) with love of one's neighbor (Lev.

19:18). In the words of the nineteenth-century German theologian Julius Wellhausen, "Jewish monotheism is belief in the almighty power of the good." The clashes and conflicts to which this belief leads in the face of the world as we actually experience it are the paradoxes for which Jewish and Christian theology have sought for answers ever since.

The wealth of interpretative possibilities is inexhaustible. That is true not only of interpretation in church and synagogue; it can also be said about the hypotheses of exegetical scholarship. This introduction offers no more than one possible outline of the history of the literature and religion of ancient Israel. Although there are good reasons for drawing the picture as I have done, this is meant only as one possible understanding. It is my hope that readers will find themselves challenged to arrive at their own judgment, the more so since the brevity of the account means that the imperatively required debate is missing. Kant formulated the Enlightenment's slogan when he said: *"Sapere aude!"*—"Have the courage to use your own reason!" If this may be applied to Holy Scripture, then it is all the more applicable where the secondary literature is in question.

Between the little book which is before the reader and the book to which it refers there is a yawning gap. This introduction can be justified only because its desire is to point to the Old Testament itself: *"Tolle lege!"*—"Pick it up and read it!" This is also a requirement because even the best explanation is in vain if the object to which it refers is unfamiliar.

Of course we cannot read the Old Testament in the way we read a novel, nor should we try to do so. It is better to open the book here and there, and to follow one's preferences. I can only point in a few directions. I might mention the gripping stories of the patriarchs; the programmatic social ethics of Deuteronomy; the exciting and yet shattering stories about the court of David; the fathomless spiritual distress of Job; the cry from the depths in the Psalms, but also their glowing praise of God and their joy in Creation; the rules for living in the book of Proverbs; the sceptical contemplation of the world in Ecclesiastes; the charming little idyll of the book of Ruth; the eroticism of the Song of Songs; the powerful sweep of the language of the prophets, and their visionary power.

In all this we can unexpectedly experience that over the gulf of thousands of years this text can address us quite directly. It can hold up a mirror to me; it can lend words for my doubts, my grieving, my joy; it can admonish me and comfort me; it can tell me to what end I can live and with what hope; tell "who the well-balanced world on hinges hung"; or say what is to be done in general, or in a particular situation.

Which translation of the Bible should one choose? For the present book my choice was the Revised Standard Version which, while taking account of advances in biblical scholarship, attempts to preserve as much as possible of the incomparable King James Version of 1611, whose phraseology and imagery exerted an unequaled influence on the English language. However, occasional changes have been made when it was important to bring out a particular nuance in the Hebrew text. An asterisk (*) following quoted or cited passages indicates a shortened or reconstructed text.

"NOT A DOT, NOR A TITTLE SHALL PASS"

The Text of the Old Testament

A book which goes back to the time before the invention of printing makes us ask about the history of its written transmission. How reliable is the version that has come down to us? What earlier versions preceded it? How far back do the testimonies which we have in black and white go? It is only if we can be sure that we have an authentic text before us that we have a basis for conclusions about the origin of what the text contains.

THE HEBREW TEXT

The oldest extant complete Hebrew manuscript of the Bible is *Codex B19A*, which is now in the public library in Saint Petersburg. It is known as the *Codex Leningradensis*, but has recently been renamed the *Codex Petropolitanus*. The scribe's colophon states that it was written in 1008 CE, in Cairo. It is also the best preserved manuscript of the whole Hebrew biblical text, and is the basis of most scholarly editions. It is excelled only by the *Aleppo Codex*, which is a few decades older, but a quarter of which has been lost since 1948.

The Aleppo and other manuscripts were written by what are known as the Masoretes, who were active from the eighth to the tenth century CE in Tiberias, on Lake Gennesaret. The Hebrew word "Masora" means "tradition," and the text passed down by these scribes is known as the *Masoretic text*. There were two leading families of scholars, the ben Asher family and the ben Naftali family. The Aleppo Codex, which served as a master copy for the preparation of other manuscripts, was vocalized by Aaron ben Asher, the Codex Petropolitanus by Samuel ben Jacob, on the basis of Aaron ben Asher's vocalization.

The impetus for this work came from the sect of the Karaites ("adherents of Scripture"), which spread from Babylonia from the eighth century onwards. The Karaites rejected the rabbinic interpretation, as passed down in the Talmud, and turned exclusively to Holy Scripture itself—a Jewish example of what Luther was later to insist on as *sola scriptura*—"through Scripture alone." Once tradition was no longer used as a help in the reading, it was important that even the most minute detail should not be in doubt. This attitude, in its turn, had a subsequent influence on rabbinic Judaism too. The Masoretes were Rabbanim.

The most important achievement of the Masoretes was the precise recording of the pronunciation. Like all Semitic alphabetical scripts, Hebrew-Aramaic is a consonantal script—that is to say, only the consonants in a word were written down. The result is a multiplicity of ambiguities and uncertainties. It is as if we were presented with the word "ht" and had to deduce from the context whether to read it as "hat", "hit", "hot" or "hut." It is true that the text never existed without a traditional pronunciation—people knew how they were expected to read it—but now the exact reading was fixed in writing through a system of vowel signs and accents: the *punctuation*.

The vocalization subjected the language which had developed in the course of centuries to a unified grammatical system. This could cause inconsistencies between the transmitted text (the *K^{e}tîb*) and the Masoretic reading (the *Q^{e}rê*). The Masoretes resorted to noting their interpretation of the consonantal text in the margin of the column. This marginal apparatus (the "small Masorah," or *"Masorah parva"*) also offered the opportunity to pass on old traditional readings as well as statistical and grammatical indications. Its main purpose, however, was to protect the text from alteration. "Masoret is a fence for the Torah," said Rabbi Aqiba (d. 135 CE). In addition to the *Masorah parva*, the *Masorah magna,* or "large Masorah," was added at the head and foot of the columns. This is an apparatus of parallel passages, compiled in the course of a long interpretative tradition.

In rabbinic Judaism, the text which emerged in this way pushed out all other versions. Manuscripts which had become unusable were not preserved, let alone used again, it being the custom to bury them solemnly; and this meant that earlier forms of the text were lost. For a long time enquiries into the pre-Masoretic textual history therefore drew a blank. The biblical quotations in the rabbinic writings showed only that the consonantal text agreed down to the smallest detail with the textual form which was the only one to be passed down in Judaism from the end of the first century CE. It was a sensational discovery in the second half of the nineteenth century which first brought about a new situation for textual study. A large number of manuscripts—an estimated 200,000 fragments—which had been forgotten and escaped destruction were discovered in the *Genizah* (Heb.: "storage place") of the Old Cairo synagogue. Today these fragments are in the University Library in Cambridge, England, and in other European and North American libraries. The oldest go back to the sixth century CE. This discovery revealed, among other things, that there were preliminary stages to the Masoretic system of vocalization.

Rabbinic Judaism was not the only religious community to hand down the Old Testament. There were also the Samaritans, who had their own shrine on Mount Garizim near Sichem. They had split off from the postexilic Jewish community at some unknown date, and kept the Torah as their Holy Scripture, though not the rest of the Old Testament. The earliest extant manuscripts of the *Samaritan Pentateuch* date from the twelfth century. Apart from some dogmatic corrections, they preserve a separate form of the text, which goes back to pre-Christian times.

THE GREEK TEXT

Hellenistic Diaspora Judaism also possessed its own version of the Old Testament: the *Septuagint*. The Latin means "seventy," and this Greek text is designated by the Roman numbers LXX (seventy). The name goes back to the legend about its origin handed down in the Letter to Aristeas, which was written in the first century BCE. According to the story, Demetrius of Phaleron, the head of the famous library in Alexandria, proposed to King Ptolemy II Philadelphus (285–246) that the Jewish laws be included in the library. For this purpose, the Torah was translated into Greek in exactly seventy-two days by seventy-two learned men, six from every tribe of Israel, whom the high priest Eleazar sent from Jerusalem to Alexandria, the translation then being approved by the Jewish congregation there. The account was given a miraculous embroidery in later Christian tradition, but may be based on historical fact to the extent that in the middle of the third century BCE the Torah was first translated into Greek for the religious needs of the Egyptian Diaspora. After that the rest of the Old Testament was gradually translated too (in different ways in the individual books). The prologue to the translation of the book of Sirach (made after 132 BCE) is aware that "the Law, the prophets, and the other books" exist in Greek.

The Septuagint differs from the Masoretic text not only in its language. The copy from which the translation has been made (the *Vorlage*) represents a different form of the text. That is particularly evident from its compass. The Septuagint includes a number of books which are missing in the Hebrew Bible. The book of Daniel and the book of Esther are much longer in the Greek version, and others, such as the book of

Jeremiah, are shorter. If we put the Greek and Hebrew texts side by side we are inescapably faced with the question: which text is the original? In the case of Holy Scripture the comparison is gunpowder, in religious terms. What is to count as revelation? It is obvious that the Hebrew text must take precedence. There are indications that even in the pre-Christian era the Greek Bible had occasionally been corrected according to the Hebrew text. But this presents textual studies with a problem: the Hebrew text which provided the basis for the corrections was not identical with the copy from which the translation had been made. So the Septuagint began early on to lose its character as representative of a separate textual form.

In the year 70 CE, with the destruction of the Second Temple, the Jewish community lost its focal point and this meant that the reference to Holy Scripture acquired all the more importance for Jewish religious identity. Judaism finally became a book religion. Consequently it was no longer possible to tolerate a multiplicity of textual forms. From this point on, reference was made solely to the version from which the Masoretic text was later derived, all others being rejected. Christians coming from Judaism, on the other hand, who appealed to the authority of Jesus Christ as well as to Scripture, did not share this exclusive understanding of Scripture, and they kept the traditional Greek Bible. It thus came about that the Septuagint was passed down only by the church, and became the Christian version of the Old Testament.

In the second century CE, new translations of the proto-Masoretic text were made for Greek-speaking

Jews in place of the Septuagint. The translation which best reflects their mentality is the *Aquila* translation, which attempts a literal rendering of the Hebrew text into Greek. From now on, just as in the rabbinic interpretation of Scripture, every detail was important theologically as being part of revelation; ultimately speaking, the sacred text cannot be translated at all. The somewhat later translations of *Symmachus* and *Theodotion* are closer than Aquila to the nature of the Greek language. But in the end the commitment to the Hebrew text was so strong that none of these translations remained in use, and except for some traces in Septuagint manuscripts they have been lost.

The relation between the Hebrew and the Greek text was not, however, elucidated just because the Jewish community abandoned the Septuagint. In the dispute about the Christological interpretation of the Old Testament, the difference acquired dogmatic importance. Although the Christians were convinced that their text had the quality of revelation, its difference from the Hebrew text of the Jews infused an uncertainty; and out of this an early form of textual criticism developed, its most masterly achievement being the *Hexapla*.

The Hexapla is a six-column Bible, compiled round about 240–245 CE, with which the great Alexandrian theologian Origen, working in Caesarea on the Palestinian coast, aimed to prove (or if necessary construct) agreement between the Greek and Hebrew texts. This gigantic work is said to have comprised fifty volumes. The Hebrew consonantal text, a Greek transliteration, the Aquila and Symmachus translations, the Septuagint, and the Theodotion translation were set side by side. On this basis, manuscripts were prepared which corrected the Septuagint according to the Hebrew text. In particular, the extra passages in the Hebrew text were inserted into the Septuagint from the Theodotion, Symmachus, or Aquila translations. These were marked by asterisks. Anything in the Greek text which was missing in the Hebrew was marked with an omission sign (*obelos*). In the course of further copying, these signs could easily drop out, the result being the "hexaplaric" text, with which the Septuagint lost its character as a form independent of the proto-Masoretic text.

Although the Hexapla has been lost except for a few fragments, Septuagint research has ways of reconstructing the original text. A translation of the edited text into Syriac, the *Syrohexapla* (616–617 CE), has preserved the text-critical marks precisely, so that it is possible to trace the process of revision in detail. The church fathers also often quote the pre-hexaplaric text in their commentaries. The great fourth-century Bible manuscripts, the *Codex Vaticanus* (now in the Vatican Library) and the *Codex Sinaiticus* (discovered in Saint Catherine's Monastery on the Sinai peninsula in 1844 and 1849, and now in Leipzig and London) show only slight editorial influence. Papyrus findings testify to the prehexaplaric textual history from the second to the fourth century. Finally, the Septuagint was already translated into the languages spoken in Christendom before the third century. Of these daughter translations, the translations into Coptic dialects made in Egypt are particularly important, as is the Latin translation used in the church of the Western Roman Empire (known as the *Vetus Latina*), although only fragments of this have survived.

OTHER TRANSLATIONS

Whereas the Septuagint has remained the Bible of the Eastern churches down to the present day, the biblical tradition of the West was determined by the *Vulgate*, the Latin translation of the Bible made by Jerome (ca. 347–420). This undertaking can be seen as a further attempt to reconcile the Hebrew text of the Jews and the Greek text of the Christians. The translation was commissioned by Pope Damasus I (366–384), and between 390 and 405 Jerome translated the whole of the Old Testament on the basis of the Hebrew text of the time—that is to say, according to the proto-Masoretic text (although the Vetus Latina still retained a certain influence). In the eighth and ninth centuries the Vulgate came to be generally accepted in the Western church. After proponents of the Reformation, under the influence of humanism, had returned to the Hebrew text, the Council of Trent declared in 1546 that the Vulgate was the authoritative text to be used by the Roman Catholic Church in matters of doctrine.

Of other translations, the most important is the Bible used by the Syriac Church, the *Peshitta* (Syr.: "the simple"). It is common to both denominations, the West Syriac Jacobites, and the East Syriac Nestorians, and therefore dates back to the period before their separation in the fifth century CE. There are well-founded reasons for assuming that the Peshitta is based on older Aramaic translations, known collectively as the *Targumim*. As Hebrew fell out of use, it became the custom in the worship of the synagogues to make the Bible text that was read comprehensible by way of an Aramaic paraphrase. This gave rise to firm traditions, and in the end these were also committed to writing. In the case of the Torah, the Targum Onqelos became authoritative, for the prophetic books the Targum Jonathan.

QUMRAN

The present state of textual study is determined by the findings made between 1947 and 1956 in the Judean desert. In the Qumran area, fifteen kilometers south of Jericho, on the Dead Sea, hidden in eleven caves, fragments of more than 190 Biblical scriptural scrolls came to light. These put our knowledge of the textual history on a new foundation. With the exception of the book of Esther, all the books of the Bible are represented, even if only in tiny fragments. Most impressive is the complete scroll of the book of Isaiah (now in the Shrine of the Book in Jerusalem). The majority of the fragments date from the second and first centuries BCE, but some go back as far as the third century BCE.

These discoveries show that round about the turn of the era, several textual forms of the Old Testament existed side by side. What is especially important is the fact that the proto-Masoretic text is also represented. This shows that this text, which was the only one used in the Jewish community from the end of the first century CE, is not an edited revision, but is also a form of the text with its own history. Some of the Qumran fragments are also close to the Samaritan form of the text. Among the earliest manuscripts, we come across some which correspond to the Hebrew Vorlage of the Septuagint. From these we can see how closely the Greek translation adhered to the Hebrew on which it was based. Finally, there are forms of the text which were hitherto unknown and for which we have evidence only in Qumran. These differ from the proto-Masoretic text through, among other things, a freer, less strict mode of transmission.

The path to the original text leads by way of a comparison between the Masoretic text (which can count as being the very best text for most of the Old Testament) and the Samaritan Pentateuch, the Qumran fragments, and above all the pre-hexaplaric Septuagint. In the case of certain books, this comparison can even show that there never was a single original text, but that the different textual forms were stages in a literary process which ultimately branched out into separate paths.

CHAPTER 2

✥

A BOOK AS LIBRARY

The Old Testament Canon

The word "Bible" goes back by way of the Latinized *biblia* to the Greek βιβλία. The word βιβλίον means "book," and βιβλία is the plural, "books." The very name therefore indicates that what we have in our hands today as a single volume and what we take as a matter of course to be a single unity, *the* Bible, is in fact a multiplicity. The Bible has often been called "the Book of Books," meaning not only the incomparability which it enjoys for the Jewish and Christian faiths, but also its inward plurality. It is, in fact, a book consisting of many books.

For a long time there was not even a term for this collection. The prologue to the translation of the book of Sirach (made after 132 BCE), which for the first time refers to it in roughly its present compass, calls it "the law, the prophets and the other books of our fathers." When the New Testament refers to the Old, it usually talks about "the law and the prophets," occasionally about "the law of Moses and the prophets and the psalms" (Luke 24:44). The threefold division indicated here corresponds to Jewish usage down to the present day: "law (*tôrāh*), prophets (*n^ebî'îm*), writings (*k^etûbîm*)," summed up as *t^enak*, an acronym, artificially formed from the first three letters. Even the name "Old Testament" does not designate the collection in itself but is a term used to differentiate it from the "New Testament"; the name came into use at the end of the second century CE, to emphasize, in opposition to the heretic Marcion, that the Holy Scripture taken over from the Jews is indispensable for the Christian faith. The fact that the Old Testament has in extent no unified contours is in line with this vagueness. The number of the books can vary according to the group that passed them down, and the arrangement of the books differs, too.

It can be said of all the versions, however, that the books they contain form a "canon." This word (Gk.: "measuring rod") is used for the collection of the writings that are viewed as authoritative revelation. From these writings, those who seek for valid answers in questions of faith can take their bearings.

THE HEBREW BIBLE

The threefold division which finds expression in the earliest designations is not merely external. It conforms both to the importance assigned to the parts, religiously speaking, and to their historical development. At the beginning is the Torah, which according to Jewish understanding is Holy Scripture per se—for the Samaritans even exclusively so. Scholars generally use the term "Pentateuch" (from the Gk.: "five-fold" [book]), since the Torah comprises the books of Genesis, Exodus, Leviticus, Numbers, and Deuteronomy, which are also numbered as the five books of Moses. They are followed by the *Prophets*. In Jewish tradition, the *historical books* of Joshua, Judges, Samuel, and Kings are considered to be "the former prophets." The prophetic books proper—Isaiah, Jeremiah, Ezekiel, and the Book of the Twelve Prophets—constitute "the latter prophets." Last of all come the *Writings*. When the Sirach prologue calls them "the other books," this shows that at the end of the second century BCE this part of the canon was not yet fully defined. It contains the latest books of the Old Testament, and it is only this part which gave rise to the debates about the admission or exclusion of individual books which the rabbis carried on in the first century CE.

The *sequence* of the books in the Torah and the former prophets was already given by the course of history, from the creation of the world until the conquest of Jerusalem. In the case of the prophetic books proper it is a different matter. The Babylonian Talmud has the sequence: "Jeremiah, Ezekiel, Isaiah, the Book of the Twelve Prophets" (Tractate Baba batra 14b). The Septuagint has this sequence: Book of the Twelve Prophets, Isaiah, Jeremiah, Ezekiel. The sequence usual in today's Bibles—Isaiah, Jeremiah, Ezekiel, Book of the Twelve Prophets—is derived from the Vulgate. In the Hebrew codices the Writings are arranged in varying ways—a further indication of how fluid the margins of the collection of sacred books had been.

THE SEPTUAGINT

The Septuagint chose a systematic order on the basis of the Hebrew canon. The decisive step was to move the prophetic books to the end. In this way the Old Testament acquired an "eschatological" finale, pointing towards the future. This was later given additional significance through the Christological interpretation. For this purpose, the Writings in the Hebrew canon have been rearranged. The book of Ruth becomes an appendix to the book of Judges, and Lamentations an appendix to the book of Jeremiah. The two books of Chronicles, Ezra, and Nehemiah follow the two books of Kings. The book of Esther is located at the end of the historical books. The apocalyptic book of Daniel here stands at the close of the prophetic books, following Ezekiel. It retains Ezekiel as neighbor in the Vulgate, too, although here the Book of the Twelve Prophets concludes the sequence. From this time on, the other five books of the Writings form a separate block, which may be called the *didactic books*, and are now placed between the historical books and the prophets: Psalms, Proverbs, Ecclesiastes, Song of Solomon, Job. The sequence of these books varies in the different manuscripts. The three parts of the canon put together in this way—the historical books (including the Torah), the didactic books, and the prophets—correspond to the three dimensions of time: past, present, future.

DEUTERO-CANONICAL WRITINGS

The Septuagint and the Vulgate include other books which no longer found acceptance within the Hebrew canon. Among the historical books, these are the Third Book of Ezra, the books of Maccabees, Tobit, and Judith; among the didactic books, they are Jesus Sirach (Ecclesiasticus) and the Wisdom of Solomon; and among the prophetic books, the book of Baruch (Jeremiah's scribe), and the Epistle of Jeremiah. There are also individual additions, such as the Prayer of Manasseh (within the second book of Chronicles), and the narrative and hymnic expansions of the books of Esther and Daniel. These surplus books are summed up under the term *Apocrypha* (Gk.: "hidden [writings]"). In the early church the term was applied to heretical books, but it now has the softened meaning of noncanonical writings. In the Protestant churches, which went back to the Hebrew canon, they were excluded. Luther called them "books not to be held equal with Holy Scripture and yet useful and profitable reading," and he placed them between the Old and New Testaments. In the Roman Catholic Church they are still an integral part of the authoritative Bible.

Families of Greek manuscripts and the Bibles of the national churches in Egypt, Ethiopia, Syria, Armenia, and Georgia contain other Jewish writings which did not achieve the rank of canonicity in the ecumenical church of the Roman Empire. Among these are the Letter of Aristeas, the Book of Jubilees, the Psalms of Solomon, the Book of Enoch, the Fourth Book of Ezra, the Testaments of the Twelve Patriarchs, and others. These writings are known as *Pseudepigrapha* (Gk.: "books falsely attributed [to their authors]"). For the religious history of Judaism in the Hellenistic and Roman periods, however, they are sources of the first importance.

CHAPTER 3

※

THE OLD TESTAMENT AS THE HOLY SCRIPTURE PASSED DOWN BY POSTEXILIC JUDAISM

THE TRANSMITTING GROUPS

The Old Testament is the Holy Scripture of the Jewish community, and the first—and by far the larger—part of the Holy Scripture of Christians. It is in the form of Holy Scripture that it has come down to us, and in order to understand it in the appropriate way we must know that it has never been anything different. Its character today as Holy Scripture characterizes its origin, as well.

The unbiased reader is bound to find this statement surprising, for it contradicts what the text itself says. Large parts of the Old Testament rather present themselves as being the record of ancient Israel's history. The historical work which comprises the books of Genesis through Kings ends with the destruction of Jerusalem by the Neo-Babylonians in the sixth century BCE—the event which according to our understanding today initiated the beginnings of the Old Testament. The Old Testament in fact begins where ancient Israel ends.

At the same time, the attentive reader will perhaps have stumbled over the first pages of the Bible: what stands at the beginning is the creation of the world. An account which starts like this from metaphysical presuppositions cannot be a record of history as such. In the Old Testament a religious community has "re-called" its past in the form of a divine history in order to win back its future.

There were literary sources for this recalling of the past, but measured against the text we have today they are few—no more than remnants, left over by a chain of historical catastrophes. It was not only the archives which fell victim to the downfall. It was also the institution for the sake of which the documents had been written down; Israel's monarchy fell in 722 BCE, and the monarchy of Judah shared the catastrophe in 586.

For its genesis, literature requires an institutional framework and a driving interest or concern. This is true especially of religious literature, and pre-eminently so in the ancient world. As far as we can see, this framework was provided for the beginnings of the Old Testament in its proper sense by the congregation of the Second Temple in Jerusalem, which the Persians had caused to be rebuilt out of the rubble between 520 and 515 BCE. It is highly probable that at this sanctuary there was both a scriptorium and a literary archive—we might even say a theological school.

THE CONCERN THAT BEGOT THE LITERATURE

The postexilic sanctuary carried on the central Judean cult under the Persian overlords, although it had lost its royal initiator and supporter. The inherent self-contradiction involved here meant that there had to be a new comprehensive interpretation of the traditional religion. This found expression in the idea of the direct sovereignty of God, a sovereignty no longer mediated through the monarchy.

This innovation was not regarded as such, however, since it served to preserve, or restore, continuity with the past. It was therefore understood as the principle that had always determined history, and the past was viewed in this light. The outcome was a comprehensive process of interpretation of the existing sources, as a result of which the living conditions of the post-national era were transported to the beginnings of the people's own history. To put it in somewhat exaggerated form: in sharp contrast to the religious history of Iron-Age Syria-Palestine, the fiction developed that Judaism had been constituted in prehistoric times, on Mount Sinai.

At the beginning this new interpretation was brought to bear on the sixth-century historical works, on the extant books of the law (Deuteronomy and the Book of the Covenant), on a basic stock of cultic lyrics and Wisdom writings, and also on the sayings of the prophets which had been committed to writing. This was not a definite event, however: in the course of the Persian and Hellenistic periods it gave rise to more and more interpretations. There were many reasons for this. The Judean cult was no longer closed and self-contained. It was exposed to the religious rivalry of the Great Powers and its own neighbors, the more so since the god Yahweh had suffered a frightful defeat with the destruction of the Temple and the loss of the

Davidic dynasty. Under the Judeans, the sanctuary now had to stand on its own, without royal protection. Once the court of King Jehoiachin had been deported to Babylon after the first conquest of Jerusalem in 597, there was a kind of Judean government in exile there: a circle of courtiers, priests, and scribes who claimed for themselves the right to interpret the Yahweh religion (and such of them as returned to Jerusalem in the course of the fifth century BCE were even able to get this interpretation generally accepted). In the course of time the Temple became the center of a worldwide Jewish community, which in the Diaspora had to preserve its faith and defend it against other religions. The old rivalry between Jerusalem and the sanctuaries in the area of the former Northern Kingdom revived. The priesthood was exposed to internal struggles about hierarchy. In the fifth and fourth centuries BCE a lower class came into being in Judah which turned against the prosperous Temple and its priesthood, claiming the support of Holy Scripture. The historical confusions of the Hellenistic period lent prophetic literature new topical relevance. People came to expect that the end of history lay ahead.

THE NATURE OF THE INTERPRETATIVE PROCESS

The origin of a Holy Scripture as a written work is the experience that an efficacious divine Word really exists. In Israel and Judah this experience was bound up with prophecy. The key event was the downfall of Jerusalem, which the prophets had prophesied as an act inflicted by the god Yahweh on his own people; at least what they had said could in retrospect be so understood. History had confirmed the prophecy. From now on what the prophets said was vouched for as the true Word of God.

People collected these prophetic sayings and began to pass them on, for their interpretation gave meaning to what had happened: the catastrophe was God's punishment. Terrible though this interpretation was, it was better than blind fate. And it offered the chance to step out of the role of mere sufferer. If the catastrophe was a punishment, the cause could be excluded in times to come through different behavior: this meant a turn to the future. The first versions of the great historical works date from about this time. Since they are a religious interpretation of history, the same traditional criteria were applied to them. From this time on, the religion lived from Scripture.

The attitude which determined the transmission of what was vouched for as being the Word of God can best be described through what is known as the "canon formula." It is a kind of certifying postscript which we find in Assyrian contracts; but it was also applied to the collections of laws in the Old Testament:

> You shall not add to the word which I command you, nor take from it; that you may keep the commandments of Yahweh your God which I command you. (Deut. 4:2; cf. 12:32).

What was demanded for the commandments was applied to the divine Word as a whole in its written form. Because it counted as normative, it was strictly unalterable.

This condition resulted in a dilemma. For Scripture was not preserved for its own sake; its purpose was to ensure that the divine Word would be valid for the present. But this is only possible if the Word is not merely handed down but is brought into discussion with the present day; and in this process it inevitably changes. There is no living reference to Scripture without interpretation.

The way out was to leave the transmitted word unchanged, but to add the interpretation. Until about the end of the Persian era, only the second half of the canon formula was applied to the Torah; nothing was taken away. The given text remained unchanged; at least it was not abridged. Nevertheless it was continually added to, and extensively so. It is only in this way that the Old Testament grew into what we now have. The core which already existed in the sixth century BCE comprised hardly more than a tenth of today's book.

The purpose of the continual process of interpretation was not to add something new and alien to the text, but to bring to light its profound meaning. An exploration of the text of this kind is called in Hebrew *midrash*. The Old Testament is distinguished from later Jewish midrash in that no distinction was made between interpretation and already existing tradition. At the next stage, in each given case, the two were presented as a unity: a single text, which was once again given an interpretation in just the same way. We might call this kind of growth a "snowball system." Once it has started rolling, the snowball picks up a new layer with every revolution. In this way the Old Testament has become to a great extent its own interpretation— *sacra scriptura sui ipsius interpres*. There is hardly a single textual unit which is not composed of several literary strata. The unit as a whole is interwoven with important cross-links to an extent that can hardly be plumbed. Recent research calls this phenomenon "intertextuality."

The growth generally took place without any rules. That was in accord with the matter at hand: a holy text is not "made"; it is received from tradition. It is merely interpreted for the needs of the present. Editorial interventions were the exception: it was rather a case of collecting, structuring, reordering, splitting book scrolls that had grown into separate units, or bundling together into a larger whole texts that belonged together.

At some point the snowball had to come to a stop. The development would otherwise have run counter to its purpose. The contours of the sacred text would have dissolved. It was for this reason that, in the end, the other half of the canon formula also came into force: "You shall add nothing." A fixed text emerged. This was not intended to put an end to the continual interpretation and actualization, nor could it do so. But from now on the interpretation ran parallel to the canonical collection that was crystallizing. It became the source of an immense secondary literature, and has remained so down to the present day.

THE LITERARY ANALYSIS

The literary analysis of the Old Testament has to do with a highly complicated object which can be fundamentally misunderstood if it is uncritically viewed as a primary source. The reference to life—and hence the point of what is said—as well as the text's status as historical source emerges only when one begins to see the depth-structure of the text as it has grown up in the historical process.

There are many different hypotheses about the way the texts came into being. Even basic facts are still in dispute. This is normal for a lively scholarly debate. However, there are a number of points which act as a safeguard against caprice, and on which the analysis can depend: breaches of form, irregular sentence structure, contradictions in content (which occasionally provoke a reaction even within the literary process itself), as well as quotations and references to other parts of Scripture. Emendations in the manuscripts—attempts at a solution made in the ancient translations as well as during the history of the interpretation—make it clear that the problems have not been imposed on the text only by modern criticism.

Because the transmitted text in its existing form was in principle inviolable, the interpreter is in the fortunate position of being able to work on the text like an archaeologist: when he removes a later stratum he may expect to come upon an earlier, intact form of the text. Dates can be arrived at through a comparison of different elements. They can relate almost exclusively to the mutual relationship of the strata and writings (relative dating). It is only in a very few cases that a date can be established through the mention of some otherwise attested historical fact. Consequently proposals diverge greatly, and have led to widely differing outlines of the literary and religious history.

CHAPTER 4

꙳

THE REMNANTS OF ANCIENT
ISRAELITE LITERATURE

With the transition from the late Bronze Age to the
Iron Age between 1200 and 1000 BCE the kingdoms of
Israel and Judah came into being in Palestine. From
that time on, we may suppose that there was a written
Hebrew culture. It is true that according to our ideas
the courts in Jerusalem and Samaria were not much
more than knightly domains, which had achieved the
status of minor states, on the basis of the power acquired by mercenary troops; but nevertheless basic
political conditions were involved. There were relations between the different courts, and that provided
the occasion for a diplomatic correspondence. There
were annals and thus the beginnings of historiography. There were taxes, and these had to be admin-
istered. For their religious legitimation, without which
no government in the ancient world existed, there was
a state cult with festivals, myths, and liturgies. Internal peace was secured by a legal system theoretically
presided over by the king, who with the powers at his
disposal guaranteed the country's internal order. And
there was a staff of literate ministerial officials, who
saw to it that all this was implemented. Among these
officials were also officially appointed priests, as well

as prophets, who claimed expert knowledge about the future.

It would be too much to say that this must already have meant the beginnings of a literature. But from this time the precondition for it existed: a caste of scribes. This little cultural elite stood in cultural continuity with the city-states of the late Bronze Age, whose correspondence with the pharaohs of the Eighteenth Dynasty (fourteenth century BCE) in Tel el-Amarna in Egypt has in part been preserved extant (ANET 483–90; COS 3.92). At this period Akkadian was the language of diplomacy; it was written on clay tablets in cuneiform script. For those who wanted to learn it, there was an educational canon, a "classical literature." A fragment of the Gilgamesh epic was found in Megiddo (ANET 72–99; COS 1.132). The epic's most famous scene, the deluge myth (ANET 42–44; COS 1.158), which goes back to third millennium Sumer, has also found its way into Hebrew literature (Gen. 6–8).

The intellectual horizon of the scribes extended beyond the borders of the individual kingdom. The status consciousness they developed can be impressively seen from Egyptian tombs. At the same time, conditions in Iron Age Palestine can hardly be too modestly imagined. The archaeological findings show that a somewhat broader written culture only existed from the seventh century BCE. Documents were written in the Old Hebrew script, a close descendent of Phoenician alphabetical writing, which was the mother of all alphabetical scripts and which was invented in the first half of the second millennium BCE. Letters, invoices, and notes were written on pottery shards (*ostraka*), leather or papyrus scrolls being used for literary texts. Unlike the clay tablets, these have been completely lost, only a few remnants surviving in the desert climate of Egypt and in the Judean desert.

WISDOM BOOKS

The scribes had a professional ethos which guided them in what they did and which for preference they took over from their professional colleagues in culturally superior Egypt. In addition they acted as advisers when political decisions had to be made. They polished their knowledge from Wisdom writings which had been handed down and which show a wealth of wise observation and knowledge of human nature.

This was the origin of Israelite Wisdom literature. Traces have survived in the earliest stratum of the book of Proverbs: in the core of the collection of "Sayings of Solomon" (Prov. 10:1–22:16), "Words of the Wise" (Prov. 22:17–24:22) with the appendix "These also are sayings of the wise" (Prov. 23–34), as well as in the collection "These also are proverbs of Solomon which the men of Hezekiah king of Judah copied" (Prov. 25–29). The ascription to Solomon establishes a link with the beginnings of the Judean monarchy, when according to the account in 1 Kings 4 public administration in Israel and Judah came into being. There may well be a grain of truth in this, although it cannot be taken literally. The mention of the men of Hezekiah (725–697 BCE) shows that the collections have a long history.

In 1924 a discovery was made which roused considerable attention. It was found that the first half of the collection "Words of the Wise" (Prov. 22:17–23:11) is closely paralleled in the Egyptian *Teachings of Amenemope*, which was written about 1100 BCE in the New Empire (ANET 421–25; COS 1.47; AEL 2.146–63). The text deals with the duties of the official, and with good manners, and it includes an admonition to be restrained in argument. The sayings have been put into the mouth of a member of the lower temple hierarchy. They are divided into thirty chapters.

> § 21: The crocodile that makes no sound, dread of it is ancient. Do not empty your belly to everyone, and thus destroy respect of you; broadcast not your words to others, nor join with one who bares his heart.

> *Compare:*
> Do not speak in the hearing of a fool, for he will despise the wisdom of your words. (Prov. 23:9)

> § 23: Do not eat in the presence of an official and then set your mouth before him; if you are sated pretend to chew, content yourself with your saliva. Look at the bowl that is before you, and let it serve your needs. An official is great in his office as a well is rich in drawing of water.

> *Compare:*
> When you sit down to eat with a ruler, observe carefully what is before you; and put a knife to your throat if you are a man given to appetite. Do

not desire his delicacies, for they are deceptive food. (Prov. 23:1–3)

Respect for the rules was important. The ancient world was realistically aware that a successful life is always endangered. Being is a little island surrounded by nonbeing, by the chaos that is a continual threat. Order is the power which preserves being against chaos. The person who orders his life in harmony with the order of existence creates the precondition for its success. Here that meant a strict observance of social barriers, but of law, too, especially the rights of the weak, the cultic order, and honesty in trade. The person who transgressed in these things was thought to be himself drawn into the whirlpool of the violated order.

The basic form of class Wisdom of this kind is the *admonition*. It can also be clothed in the form of a stated fact. A particular moral or immoral, wise or foolish kind of behavior is named (no strict line being drawn here between morality and Wisdom),and the consequences are described as a fact of experience:

> Whoever loves discipline loves knowledge,
>
> but he who hates reproof is stupid. (Prov: 12:1)

The borderline between the class Wisdom of the scribes and courtiers and the generally accepted rules of upbringing which determine family life ("clan Wisdom") is fluid; and the court at that time must in general not be thought of as all too far removed from the living conditions of the ordinary person.

The classic genre of didactic sayings of this kind is the *proverb*. Its impact and memorability is intensified through *poetry*. As everywhere, the stylistic means are rhythm and rhyme. Ancient Hebrew *prosody* still presents us with some puzzles even today, since we lack the bridge to the living language. The most plausible hypothesis is the stress theory, according to which every essential unit of meaning is given a stress. It emerges from this that the double-trio (3 + 3) and the quintet (3 + 2 or 2 + 3) are the commonest meters. The precondition is the poetic interplay of at least two sentences or part-sentences. This pair of sentences forms a *thought couplet* (this is technically called *parallelismus membrorum*). The two (or more) lines play on one and the same thought under different aspects. This characterizes all Ancient Near Eastern poetry, and it can be fascinating. In simplified form, a distinction is made between the synonymous parallelism (where the first statement is repeated, with variation) and the antithetical parallelism (where the first statement is intensified through the negation of its opposite). In addition there is the climactic parallelism, or staircase-parallelism, in which the statement is in part repeated and thus extended.

The comparison of conditions and phenomena belongs to the observation of the world in Wisdom.

> As a door turns on its hinges, so does a sluggard on his bed. (Prov. 26:14)

The evaluation takes the form of "better than" sayings:

> Better is a neighbor who is near than a brother who is far away. (Prov. 27:10)

It is better to live in a corner of the housetop than
in a house shared with a contentious woman.
(Prov. 21:9; 25:24)

Better is a dinner of herbs where love is than a fat-
ted ox and hatred with it. (Prov. 15:17)

It was not just rules of conduct which were passed on.
Astonished observation led on to *the beginnings of sci-
ence*, a phenomenology whose results are set down in
comparative and classifying lists. We have lists of this
kind in the "Words of Agur" (Prov. 30:1–33):

Three things are too wonderful to me; four I do not
understand: the way of an eagle in the sky, the way
of a serpent on a rock, the way of a ship on the
high seas, and the way of a man with a maiden.
(Prov. 30:18–19)

Four things on earth are small, but they are exceed-
ingly wise: the ants are a people not strong, yet
they provide their food in the summer; the badgers
are a people not mighty, yet they make their homes
in the rocks; the locusts have no king, yet all of
them march in rank; the lizard you can take in your
hands, yet it is in kings' palaces. (Prov. 30:24–28)

Impressive *observations of nature* can be found in
God's speeches in the book of Job (Job 38:1–39:30;
40:6–41:26). These present a kind of zoological kalei-
doscope. Not only lions, wild oxen, and ostriches, but
also the hippopotamus ("Behemoth") and the crocodile ("Leviathan") are described in a way that shows
that they have been exactly observed. Since neither

hippopotamus nor crocodile can be found in Palestine, Egyptian influence leaps to the eye. Even real *theories about the origin of the world* were known, theories which in their degree of abstraction approach pre-Socratic philosophy. It is a theory of this kind that is behind the account of Creation on the first page of the Bible (Gen. 1).

ANNALS AND HISTORIOGRAPHY

Up to now, apart from a few lists of doubtful date naming districts and officials (e.g., Josh. 15; 1 Kings 4), only a number of ostraka have survived, recording government business and correspondence at the courts of Jerusalem and Samaria. These ostraka give us a limited insight into the administration of taxes and into military affairs. The compilation of *annals* was undoubtedly one of the scribe's tasks. In these, important public events were recorded as well as the succession and reigns of the kings. Such information provided the foundation for the calendar and for a simple historiography. In the books of Kings the editors regularly refer readers to the existing archives. It would seem that many of the details which the books of Kings report—through the use of a few catchwords—have been drawn from these sources. Cross-references to the history of Mesopotamia and Egypt provide us with the basis for an exact chronology from the ninth century onwards.

Annals were compiled for the Temple, too. Among other things these preserve the sanctuary's current financial position. That is the reason why they are frequently mentioned in the books of Kings. From this source we learn about a number of military campaigns and wars: the campaign of Pharaoh Shoshenk (945–924 BCE) in Palestine (1 Kings 14:25–26); the border war between Israel and Judah in the ninth century BCE (1 Kings 15:17–22); the wars with the Arameans (2 Kings 12:18–19), the war between Joash of Israel and Amaziah of Judah (2 Kings 14:8–14), the campaign of Aram and Israel against Judah in 734–733 BCE (2 Kings 16:5, 7–9); and the siege of Jerusalem by Sennacherib of Assyria in 701 (2 Kings 18:13–15). Even the records of the two captures of Jerusalem by the Neo-Babylonians in 597 and 586 are preserved in this source (2 Kings 24–25).

The great *historical narratives* preserved in the books Judges through Kings are very different in kind. Their setting and the dramatis personae show that they belong to the Northern Kingdom of Israel, where an extremely advanced literary culture evidently existed. These texts are the best examples of ancient Hebrew prose that have come down to us. They include the story about the murder of the Moabite king Eglon, in Judges 3; the story about the kingdom of Abimelech, in Judges 9; the greater part of the stories about Saul, David, and Solomon, in 1 Samuel 11 to 1 Kings 1; the stories about the wars with the Arameans, 1 Kings 20, 22 and 2 Kings 6–7; the account of the campaign against Moab, 1 Kings 3; and lastly, and especially impressively, the account of Jehu's putsch, 2 Kings 9–10. In their virtuoso sequence of scenes and their dramatic dialogues these stories are unparalleled in ancient Near Eastern literature.

Their very subjects make it clear that these narratives are "courtly" literature, showing the self-understanding of reigning military leaders, which is what the kings of Israel and Judah always remained. The aim is to legitimate their knightly prowess and set it in a heroic light. The striking event is at the center. Such anecdotes are historical sources only indirectly at best. The causes and wider connections are beyond their horizon. Occasionally there are passages of real propaganda, like the story of Naboth's vineyard (1 Kings 21:1–16*), which attributes a judicial murder to King Ahab and his Phoenician wife, Jezebel, in order to justify the bloody end of the house of Ahab brought about by Jehu's putsch (845 BCE).

The present books Judges through Kings are probably based on *collections* and narrative cycles. As mentioned, most of the stories derive from the Northern Kingdom of Israel. When the Assyrians conquered Samaria in 722, the texts must have been brought to Judah by courtiers who had fled the country. It is only in this way that we can explain how they survived and, from the sixth century BCE, found a place in the emerging Old Testament.

LAW BOOKS

Old Testament law in the written form in which it has been passed down to us also goes back to court sources, even though for the most part we have to look for its origins elsewhere. The law was generally practiced locally, when full citizens, according to tradition, decided matters under dispute in the assembly in the gate. They also saw to it that revenge, which as "socially normative private punishment" took the place of a public prosecution, remained within bounds:

> Life for life, eye for eye, tooth for tooth, hand for hand, foot for foot, burn for burn, wound for wound, stripe for stripe. (Exod. 21:23–25)

This *ius talionis* (Lat.: "law of equivalence") is actually the foundation for a well-ordered criminal law, because it confines the punishment to the injury that has really been inflicted. Of course the precise identity between act and punishment is somewhat of a postulate. In actual practice the ius talionis probably provided the basis for compensation claims.

Most conflicts belonged to the sphere of civil law. As a basis for decisions, an elaborate system of common law developed. A long tradition of precedents was passed down. These crystallized into legal pronouncements with an "if/then" structure: act and consequence, case and verdict. The term for this is *case law*:

> When one man's ox hurts another's, so that it dies, then they shall sell the live ox and divide the price of it; and the dead beast also they shall divide. Or if it is known that the ox has been accustomed to gore in the past, and its owner has not kept it in, he shall pay ox for ox, and the dead beast shall be his. (Exod. 21:35–36)

Legal principles of this kind are not peculiar to Israel. There are many correspondences in law collections such as the ancient Babylonian Code of Hammurabi (ANET 163–80; COS 2.131), the Laws of Eshnunna (ANET 161–63; COS 2.130), the middle Assyrian, (ANET 180–88; COS 2.132), Hittite (ANET 188–97; COS 2.133) and Neo-Babylonian laws (ANET 197–98; COS 2.133). The parallels are extremely important for legal history, not least because of the details in which they deviate from one another and from Israelite law.

The earliest Israelite collection is preserved in Exodus 20:22–23.33, the so-called *Book of the Covenant*. It has a nucleus of case law (Exod. 21:1–22:16*) which probably once constituted a law book of its own. What has been put together here, however, is far from an exhaustive legal system. The subject is compensation and bodily injury, and even that is very incomplete.

Why was the ancient traditional law codified in a selection like this? A possible reason emerges from the example of the Code of Hammurabi. There, by way of a prologue and epilogue, the collection of legal provisions is given the formal framework of a royal inscription. The code served the king's political self-presentation, but was evidently not designed for practical legal purposes. The king appropriated the law that had been handed down (and which perhaps already existed in thematically limited collections), but he was not as a rule concerned with its implementation. His aim was to present himself as the guardian of "law and justice." We may presume that something similar was also true of the kings of Israel and Judah, even if the Book of the Covenant does not have—or perhaps no longer has—any such framework.

To establish the king's law was probably also the purpose of *Deuteronomy* in its original form, a form preserved in the nucleus Deuteronomy 12–26. It was very probably occasioned by the religious policy of King Josiah (639–609). Josiah concentrated the official Yahweh cult in Jerusalem, but prohibited it in the rest of the country. This was probably for political reasons: he wanted to increase his own power, and to avert the possible competition of the Yahweh shrines in the former Northern Kingdom. This concentration of the cult required a reorganization of matters which had hitherto been the affair of the local Yahweh shrines. Rules were laid down about sacrificial practice, about the great cultic feasts held during the year, about provision for the cultic personnel, and about the administration of justice. These things form the basis of Deuteronomy. In the background is the wording of the Book of the Covenant, so that we may talk about an amended law. This can hardly have taken any form other than a royal edict. The account in 2 Kings 22–23 explains Josiah's cultic policy by saying that the king obeyed the Torah, which had been (re)discovered during repairs to the Temple. But this is a legend.

CULTIC LYRICS

The court and the sanctuary established there were the scene of the official *cult*. The king maintained the cultic site and, as vassal of the Deity, he played the key part in the practice of the cult. The priests were his servants. But of course religious practice was not confined to the royal sanctuary.

The occasions for cultic practices can be divided (to put it in simplified terms) into the regular and the extraordinary. The regular occasions were focused on the seasons of the year and the cycles of the harvest, and the rites were performed by the local community. The special occasions had to do with the fate of the individual and took place in the family: pregnancy, birth, the weaning of a child, coming of age, marriage, illness, and death. The local and the family cults each had their own form, and these differed from what we know from the written testimonies about the court cult. The multiplicity of idols and inscriptions uncovered by archaeologists in recent times give witness to ideas about God which have proved a considerable surprise to biblical scholars. For it was almost exclusively the religion of the court which influenced the written records. It was only the official cult that offered the possibility and the occasion for written testimonies to the religion practiced. Of course we should not draw too hard and fast a line between family religion, local cults, and the court. It might even be said that in the religion of the court the different levels intersected. The king's personal fate was held to be the necessary condition for public order and welfare.

The occasion for celebrating this in the cult was the king's *accession*. Since natural and political conditions were expressed in myth, this occasion was celebrated in the cult as God's own ascent to the throne. This probably took place in an annual rhythm. The seasons in Palestine are marked by stark contrasts. During the summer drought there is practically no rain at all, so the land becomes parched. But in the autumn, dramatic thunderstorms, awaited with both hope and fear, usher in the winter rains. These storms are accompanied by violent autumnal gales over the Mediterranean. The Ugarit epics, especially the Baal cycle, written in the fourteenth century BCE (ANET 129–42; COS 1.86), show that this abrupt change was interpreted as the struggle of the gods for royal supremacy. The myth tells that in summer, the god of death vanquished the weather god, who disappeared from the earth. With the coming of the winter rains, the weather god began his reign once more, after a dramatic struggle in which he had won the victory over the chaotic sea god, who was the enemy of life.

> Yahweh has become king!
> He is robed in majesty,
> Yahweh is robed,
> he is girded with strength. . . .
> *The floods have lifted up, Yahweh,*
> *the floods have lifted up their voice. . . .*
> *Mightier than the thunders of many waters,*
> *mightier than the waves of the sea*
> *Yahweh on high is mighty, . . .*
> *Yahweh for evermore.* (Ps. 93*)

"Floods," "waters," and "sea" are the quintessence of the destructive forces which beat against the earth from every side. The experience that these forces of chaos are controlled and kept in check is equated with the founding and preservation of the cosmos, that is to say with Creation. It is true that the Old Testament has not preserved the myths itself, but the earliest *hymns* in the Psalter indirectly give us an impression of the drama played out in the cult. In Jerusalem (and Samaria) the weather god Yahweh enjoyed a certain programmatic exclusivity, as the god of state and dynasty. He is the local form of the deity who was worshipped in other places under the names Hadad, Adad, or Baal. Just as political rivals were expected to subordinate themselves to the king, so the rival gods were expected to subject themselves to the god Yahweh. It is still a long way from this religion, which was related to the natural and political order, to the later exclusive worship of Yahweh, but nevertheless the path has been struck out. It was not for nothing that the postexilic cult used the ancient hymns as a way of extolling Yahweh's direct royal rule.

Apart from hymns of this kind, the *laments* and the related songs of trust and thanksgiving constitute the earliest stock of psalms. They, too, have their roots in kingship. Their attribution to "David" indicates the official occasion for which they were composed, although this should not of course be understood as a statement of authorship.

> How long, Yahweh? Will you forget me for ever?
> How long will you hide your face from me?
> How long must I hold counsels in my soul,
> and have sorrow in my heart all the day?
> How long shall my enemy be exalted over me?
> Consider and answer me, Yahweh, my God;
> lighten my eyes, lest I sleep the sleep of death;

lest my enemy say, "I have prevailed over him";
lest my foes rejoice because I am shaken.
But I have trusted in your steadfast love,
my heart shall rejoice in your salvation.
I will sing to Yahweh,
because he has dealt bountifully with me. (Ps. 13)

The situation of the human being as he stands before God is described as if it were a royal audience. This is what is behind the motif about the hiding or showing of the face; it means the admission or rejection of the petitioner. The deity called upon is conceived of in the image of the king (and warrior). Very probably the original petitioner for whom these poetic formularies were written was the king; for it is just as the ordinary citizen and vassal behaves to the king that the petitioner behaves to his heavenly overlord.

What also speaks in favor of this supposition is the situation: a threatening enemy. This is by no means merely a projection of general anxieties, or the expression of some random crisis. The enemy has the features of the military opponent, and the conflict is described like a real duel. It is easy to see that the men at court might soon have taken over prayers drawn up for the cult's royal lord and used them in their own personal crises. Ultimately speaking, these were formulations available to every participant in the cult when he brought his concerns before the Deity at the sanctuary. In this way critical legal situations and illness were added to the assaults of the enemy. Sumerian, Babylonian, and Assyrian prayers also already shift between the fear of enemies, legal difficulties, and sickness. The biblical psalms, which still profoundly influence the prayer of the Christian church as well, are by no means unique in the history of religion.

The sequence of the liturgy can also be reconstructed according to the pattern of Mesopotamian sources. As a rule the lament was associated with a sacrifice. If the sacrifice was accepted, the prayer was thought to have been heard. The response was proclaimed in a *salvation oracle*. We have oracular answers to prayer of this kind in written form dating from the period of the Assyrian kings Esarhaddon (681–669 BCE) and Assurbanipal (669–631 BCE).

> Esarhaddon, king of the countries, fear not! Your enemies, like a wild boar in the month of Sivan, from before your feet will flee away. I am the great divine lady, I am the goddess Ishtar of Arbela, who will destroy your enemies from before your feet. What are the words of mine, which I spoke to you, that you did not rely upon? I am Ishtar of Arbela. I shall lie in wait for your enemies, I shall give them to you. I, Ishtar of Arbela, will go before you and behind you: fear not! (ANET 449–50)

These oracles have the same form, even in precise details, as the oracles of salvation in the second part of the book of Isaiah (Isa. 41:8–13; 43:1–7), behind which we have every reason for seeing the priest's response to the lament.

The oracle of salvation is answered by the *song of trust*. We can almost see how the king, having received the assurance of salvation, appears before the assembled troops and passes on the good tidings, in order to encourage them:

> Yahweh is my light and my salvation:
> whom shall I fear?
> Yahweh is the stronghold of my life;
> of whom shall I be afraid? . . .
> Though a host encamp against me,
> my heart shall not fear;
> though war arise against me,
> yet I will be confident. . . .
> For he will hide me in his shelter, . . .
> he will set me high upon a rock.
> And now my head shall be lifted up
> above my enemies round about me.
> (Ps. 27A*; cf. Pss. 3; 23; 118:6–7, 10–13)

The deliverance is followed by the *song of thanksgiving*, again sung at the cultic place. Here is an example: a thanksgiving for healing after a life-threatening illness:

> I will extol you, Yahweh, for y7awn me up,
> and have not let my foes rejoice over me.
> Yahweh, my God, I cried to you for help,
> and you have healed me.
> Yahweh, you have brought up my soul from Sheol,
> restored me to life from among those gone down to
>   Sheol.
> You have turned for me my mourning into dancing;
> you have loosed my sackcloth
> and girded me with gladness,

that my soul may praise you and not be silent.
Yahweh, my God, I will give thanks to you for ever.
(Ps. 30:1–3, 11–12)

PRIESTS AND PROPHETS

For the practice of the cult, "professionals" were
needed, who were expert in interpreting the will of
the Deity. All sizeable sanctuaries in the country were
run by *priests*. The sacred precinct was in their cus-
tody, they guarded the statue of the god, decided
whether the sacrifice was properly carried out, were
available to give advice to those who expected help
from God, such as healing or a divine judgment, and
they lived from the people's offerings. The sanctuary
was their benefice. A benefice of this kind could quite
well be bequeathed to the next generation, and the
priesthood tended to become a caste. The priestly office was traditionally exercised by certain families.

In ancient times the Levites were prominent. We can
see from the stories about Moses (Exod. 2–4) their
sense of their position. According to his name, Moses
was of Egyptian origin (cf. the names of the pharaohs
in the Seventeenth to the Twentieth Dynasty: Kamose,
Ahmose, Thutmose, Ramses). But on both his father's
and his mother's side he was declared to be a Levite,
and was supposed to have been brought up by the
pharaoh's daughter. The story that his mother had exposed him by putting him in a basket in the river
(Exod. 2:1–10*) echoes a theme known to us in similar
form from Neo-Assyrian sources, in the legend about

the birth of Sargon I (c. 2370 BCE), the legendary founder of the Early Akkadian Empire (see ANET 119; COS 1.133).

Like the benefices themselves, professional knowledge was also passed down in the priestly families. There was no need for a codified priestly rule. But it seems that there were also written sources behind the sacrificial regulations in Leviticus 1–7, the purity requirements in Leviticus 11–15, and the ordeal instructions in Numbers 5, the essential core of these requirements being age-old tradition.

Along with the priests there were *prophets*. The functions of the two groups cannot always be clearly distinguished, since divination also made use of the inspection of the entrails of sacrificial animals among other things, and since the priests also made predictions. Prophecy exists always and everywhere. All planning depends on prediction, especially in times of crisis, whether personal or in times of war. Whereas in Babylonia and Assyria, Egypt, and Greece divination based on external signs predominated, it is inspirational prophecy that is characteristic of Israel.

In the later period the word *prophet* (Heb.: *nābî'*) became the collective term for "men of religion" of many different kinds; for the prophet counted as the medium per se of revelation. It was already known that this was a later development of the term's meaning: "He who is now called a prophet was formerly called a seer" (1 Sam. 9:9). The explanatory comment occurs in the tradition about Samuel. In origin, Samuel was the pupil of a priest, and had been dedicated to the sanctuary by his mother (1 Sam. 1–3).

When Saul comes looking for his father's asses, who had run away, he claims Samuel as a seer (1 Sam. 9), and on the same occasion Samuel acts as exponent of political religion: he anoints Saul king in Yahweh's name.

We meet another kind of prophet in the person of Elijah. According to the frame-story in 1 Kings 17–18*, he comes to the fore as a rainmaker. Samaria has been stricken by a drought lasting several years, which is put down to a command of Elijah's. The king and his steward search the country from end to end, looking for water. Then Elijah comes forward and promises the king that rain will soon return.

Later a programmatic scene was interpolated into this story, describing the contest between Baal and Yahweh about a sacrifice, Elijah here being the central figure. The contest issues in the public proof: "Yahweh is God!" Since this is the Hebrew meaning of the name *'eliyyāhû*, it is this story of all others which can be accounted an authentic Elijah tradition. It was evidently at this time that in Samaria there really was a turn to Yahweh as dynastic God. With the second generation of the Omride dynasty, among the kings of Israel (and soon among the kings of Judah, too) proper names incorporating the name *Yahweh* begin to be used. It is difficult to date the Elijah tradition precisely, however, since the stories probably became part of the books of Kings at a later date.

The same can be said of a second narrative cycle, the stories about Elisha (2 Kings 2; 3:4–8:15; 9:1–10; 13:14–21). Elisha was a miracle-worker, and the head of a guild of so-called prophet's disciples. Brief, anecdotal miracle stories tell how with supernatural means he helped his disciples in critical situations. Elisha seems also to have been more politically active than Samuel and Elijah. In the account of Jehu's putsch, one of Elisha's disciples anoints Jehu king, as an assertion that the usurper has been authorized by Yahweh. These three representatives of preliterary prophets were closely associated with the monarchy.

There were also prophets who fulfilled an official function at the court and at the sanctuary belonging to it. The title *nābî'* was probably originally associated with this function. The prophet Nathan (1 Kings 1), one of the key figures in the Court History of David, was a *cultic prophet* of this kind. We may assume that many more occupied this position than we know of from what has been passed down to us. The king consulted them before enacting important state business. They came before the Deity as intercessors in the name of the king, the people, or individuals. They also spoke out on their own account.

Of the representatives of Old Testament *written prophecy*, Nahum seems to have been a cultic prophet. It was Nahum who proclaimed the forthcoming destruction of the Assyrian capital, Nineveh (612 BCE). The book of Habakkuk can also be understood in a similar sense, provided that we assume that his message was directed against the Neo-Babylonians (Hab. 2). Inasmuch as they prophesied disaster to the country's enemies, the prophets proclaimed the salvation of their own people. This was normal practice.

It would seem that *Isaiah* was also a cultic prophet. He received his call in the temple in Jerusalem. This event, which is dated as occurring in the year that King Uzziah died (736 BCE), is reported in Isaiah 6 as a legitimation account. The prophet sees God on his throne, his terrible royal glory filling the Temple and the whole world of the living. Winged serpent-like beings (seraphs) accompany him and begin to sing the liturgy, in which the adoration of the heavenly beings intermingles indistinguishably with the song of worshippers in the temple. Faced with this vision, the prophet, appalled, recognizes his impurity and knows that he must die. But one of the seraphs comes forward out of the sphere of terror and touches the prophet's lips with a live coal. After his mouth has thus been purified, Isaiah receives Yahweh's commission and is, from that time on, his authentic voice.

The message he has to pass on can best be understood through the symbolic name he gives his son.

> Then Yahweh said to me, "Take a large tablet and write upon it in common characters, *Maher-shalal-hash-baz* ('The spoil speeds, the prey hastens')." . . . And I went to the prophetess, and she conceived and bore a son. Then Yahweh said to me, "Call his name *Maher-shalal-hash-baz*; for before the child knows how to cry 'My father' or 'My mother,' the wealth of Damascus and the spoil of Samaria will be carried away before the king of Assyria." (Isa. 8:1, 3–4)

Yahweh announces a threat which the prophet passes on in double form. First Isaiah writes the slogan "*Maher-shalal-hash-baz*" on a great tablet. The fact that the threat is given a fixed written form has a documentary significance—perhaps even a magic one. This may be one explanation (among many others) why and how prophetic sayings have been committed to writing.

In a second step, Isaiah puts a living sign into the world. He begets a son with "the prophetess," whose title shows that she, too, had an official position at the sanctuary. The oracle that is then spoken repeats the threatening slogan, as the name to be given to the coming child. It now becomes plain against whom the threat is directed and it is given a temporal perspective: by the time that the boy begins to speak, Assyria will have destroyed the two states of Aram ("Damascus") and Israel ("Samaria"). This prophecy was probably occasioned by a campaign waged by Aram and Israel against Jerusalem in 734 or 733 BCE (cf. 2 Kings 16:5, 7–9). The prediction that the two enemies will soon be destroyed was realistic, in view of the Assyrian thrust towards expansion. For Judah, the prediction was a hopeful one: a calculated political prophecy of salvation. The cultic prophet proclaims God's judgment on the country's enemies.

It would seem that the prophecy of *Hosea* was prompted by the same event. The first three chapters of the book, which tell of Hosea's symbolic marriage with a whore, can hardly have been composed independently of Isaiah's sign. Their core, in Hosea 1*, seems like a triple copy of the symbolic action in Isaiah 8:

> Yahweh said to Hosea, "Go, take to yourself a wife of harlotry and have children of harlotry, for the land commits great harlotry by forsaking Yahweh."
> So he went and took Gomer, the daughter of

Diblaim, and she conceived and bore him a son. And Yahweh said to him, "Call his name Jezreel; for yet a little while, and I will punish the house of Jehu for the blood of Jezreel." . . . She conceived again and bore a daughter. And Yahweh said to him, "Call her name Not pitied, for I will no more have pity on the house of Israel, to forgive them at all." . . . When she had weaned Not pitied, she conceived and bore a son. And Yahweh said, "Call his name Not my people, for you are not my people and I am not your God."

This time the threat is directed solely against the Northern Kingdom of Israel, and it is spoken as an unequivocal announcement of Yahweh's punishment. In the case of "The spoil speeds, the prey hastens," the child as its speech develops becomes the embodied threat for Judah's enemies. Hosea's children, on the other hand, are mere name-bearers. The incorporating of a threat into a name has become a topos. Here the choice of mother is also symbolic: as a whore she stands for Israel's whorish apostasy, its abandonment of Yahweh. The guilt is defined as the blood guilt of Jezreel—probably a reference to the fact that in Jehu's putsch a number of Judean princes lost their lives (2 Kings 10:12–14). This, however, was a mere pretext, since the event had taken place over a century earlier. Again the message can be better explained in the context of the contemporary military conflict. The fact that Israel was at daggers drawn with Judah could not be reconciled with the worship in both states of the same dynastic God. Consequently the prophecy maintains that Yahweh hates Israel, and has put an end to his bond with it. Judah claims the god Yahweh for itself alone, in order to have his support against the enemy's attack. It is unlikely that this prophecy originated in the North, as the tradition for obvious reasons maintains. Hosea was another Isaiah.

As the place he came from shows, the prophet Amos of Tekoa was a Judean. *Amos*'s message—if we again judge by its central utterance—is so close to the proclamation of Isaiah and Hosea that it too can best be understood in the context of the warlike conflict between Israel and Judah. The dating associates the prophet with King Jeroboam II (787–747 BCE); but this is fictitious. The interpretation of his message may be a matter of controversy, but what is unambiguous is that Amos as a Judean pronounced judgment on Israel, and did so in the eighth century BCE, when the name "Israel" did not yet designate God's people, but was the name of the Northern Kingdom:

> Thus Yahweh showed me: behold, a basket of summer fruit (*qayiṣ*). And he said, "Amos, what do you see?" And I said, "A basket of summer fruit (*qayiṣ*)." Then Yahweh said to me, "The end (*qeṣ*) has come upon my people Israel." (Amos 8:1–2)

This fourth (and originally sole) vision in the book depends on an assonance between two keywords. What Amos sees is a kind of still life, which in itself evokes positive associations. When Yahweh tells him to name what he sees, "summer fruit" (*qayiṣ*) evokes the similar-sounding *qeṣ*, "end." The interpretation then emerges as if self-evident: "The end has come upon my people

Israel." This is the point of Hosea's symbolic action, too, in different words: "You are not my people and I am not your God." The difference is only that where Hosea announces Yahweh's direct punitive act, "I will punish . . . ," in Amos, as in Isaiah, the prediction is indirect. It was Amos's "No," originally hurled at hostile Israel from Judah—and therefore meant as a prophecy of salvation—which a century and a half later showed itself to be the interpretative key to the catastrophe of the South, as well (cf. Jer. 1:11–14; Jer. 24; Ezek. 7), and established the theological meaning of prophecy.

Jeremiah, the last of the great pre-exilic prophets, also supports Judean policy, even if in a more differentiated way. He criticizes King Jehoiakim and advises and warns King Zedekiah. Apparently, for a time before the city was finally conquered, he was drawn into the conflicts between the different parties at court. We learn this from the story in Jeremiah 37–38, which tells that as a result he was temporally imprisoned in the guard house.

The earliest saying of Jeremiah to which we can put a date has to do with the tragic end of King Josiah, who lost his life at Megiddo, in the battle against the pharaoh Neco (Jer. 22:10). The Judeans put Jehoahaz on the throne; but the pharaoh carried him off to Egypt and installed Jehoiakim as king. Jeremiah declares that Jehoahaz's fate is irreversible. He is fiercely critical of Jehoiakim, the vassal of the victorious power:

> Woe to him who builds his house by unrighteousness, and his upper rooms by injustice. . . . Do you

think you are king because you compete in cedar?
Did not your father eat and drink and do justice
and righteousness? Then it was well with him.
(Jer. 22:13–15*)

Jehoiakim's father, Josiah, has counted ever since as
the model of the good king. But even more characteristic of Jeremiah than political utterances of this kind
are the sayings about the enemy from the North. Once
they had defeated Egypt at Carchemish (605 BCE), the
Neo-Babylonians had possessed supreme power over
Palestine. Nebuchadnezzar conquered Jerusalem for
the first time in 597. Jehoiachin and his court were deported and Zedekiah was installed as compliant vassal. After his rebellion, the second conquest followed
in 586, ending in the annihilation of the dynasty, the
Temple, and the city's fortifications.

> A lion has gone up from his thicket,
> a destroyer of nations has set out. . . .
> A hot wind from the bare heights in the desert
> toward the daughter of my people,
> not to winnow or cleanse. . . .
> Behold, he comes up like clouds,
> his chariots like the whirlwind;
> his horses are swifter than eagles—
> woe to us, for we are ruined! (Jer. 4*)

This powerful and moving poetry is not really a
prophecy; it is a lament. The political disaster is con-
nected with the social catastrophe. What the lament
attacks is the decline in morality and in mutual trust
(Jer. 5:1–6*; 9:1–9*). General helplessness is spreading

(Jer. 8:4–7*). How far this is really prediction and how far the disaster has already taken place is hard to decide, especially since the catastrophe overtook the country in various stages between 609 and 586 BCE. In contrast to the prophecy of Hosea, the author of the disaster is the "enemy from the North," never Yahweh. The reproach that the Judeans had turned away from their god Yahweh is completely missing.

Chapter 5

※❀※

The Great Redactions of the Sixth Century bce

The fact that the remnants of ancient Israelite literature have been preserved for us is due especially to two edited compilations made soon after the conquest of Jerusalem: the Yahwist's and the Deuteronomistic history. Both are reactions to the political and religious catastrophe, although in different, indeed opposing, ways. Neither work has survived as a separate entity in today's Old Testament. The Yahwist's history forms the earliest redactional level of the books Genesis through Numbers, the Deuteronomistic history is the first continuous redaction of the books Deuteronomy through Kings. Both are hypotheses.

The Yahwist's History

Eighteenth-century exegesis already detected that the beginning of the Bible has been compiled from two sources. The story of Creation is told twice (Gen. 1 and Gen. 2). There are two genealogies of Adam's descendants (Gen. 4 and Gen. 5). In the Flood narrative, two accounts are interwoven, and the details of the two are irreconcilable (Gen. 6–8). This observation was later extended to the whole of the Pentateuch and even beyond. It was so convincing that it was again applied to the two sources themselves, and it came to be assumed that there were other similar sources, too. Among these the "Elohist" (E) found wide acceptance, although a third strand cannot in fact be convincingly traced. The two-source hypothesis has proved itself as far as the books of Genesis, Exodus, and Numbers are concerned.

The earlier of the two written sources is known in exegetical studies by the code name "Yahwist" (J), because it uses the name *Yahweh* for God from the outset, whereas according to the other Pentateuch source, the "Priestly source" (P), the name was only made known later, through a revelation to Moses (Exod. 6). For a long time the work was viewed as a narrative composition which had drawn on oral tradition. In recent times the inner lack of unity, which had already been noticed in the nineteenth century, was explained on the basis of editorial history. The Yahwist is a compilation which has welded together already existing written sources into a new whole, under a unified viewpoint.

The primeval history, Genesis 1–11, is based on a didactic narrative about the origin of mankind. God creates the first man and plants a garden in Eden for him. He creates the animals, and the woman from the man's rib (Gen. 2–3). The two have a son, Cain. A sequence of ten generations, into which various notes about the development of cultural skills are interpolated (Gen. 4), leads over in Genesis 10 to a list of the peoples of the world, as it was then known from a Palestinian viewpoint, classifying them according to their domicile. This may perhaps be a description of the world as it was in the seventh century BCE. Into this thread the story about the Flood was later inserted: in this catastrophe all life is again destroyed. Only Noah is left, and with him the history of mankind begins afresh. The sequence which thus emerges—the creation of human beings, their destruction, and their ultimate preservation—can already be found in the Old Babylonian Atramhasis epic (ANET 104–6; COS 1.130).

The stories about the patriarchs, Genesis 12–15, are essentially the story of a family. Abraham, Isaac, and Jacob are grandfather, father, and son. The great narratives on which the sequence of events rests deal with the happenings which are of fundamental importance for the family's existence: the wooing of a bride and marriage (Gen. 24; 29), the birth of sons (Gen. 16; 21; 29–30), and the struggle for the legacy (Gen. 27). What is striking is the wide geographical dispersion. Abraham settles in the steppe, near Egypt (Gen. 20:1), Isaac in Beersheba (Gen. 28:10). But the country where their relatives live, from where Isaac takes his wife (Gen. 24) and to which Jacob flees from his brothers (Gen. 29), is north Syria.

This family story has subsequently been molded into a kind of *story about national origins.* Jacob and Esau are now considered to be the tribal fathers of Israel and Edom. Jacob founds the national sanctuary of the Northern Kingdom in Bethel (Gen. 28), gives the mountains of Gilead their name (Gen. 31), and founds Mahanaim in Transjordan (Gen. 32), as well as Luz and Rachel's burial place near Ephrat (Gen. 35). What is striking is that all these episodes are localized in the Northern Kingdom, but that the kings play no part in them. It is possible that the attempt to regain history through this narrative is the work of members of the upper class who fled to Judah after the fall of Samaria.

The oldest form of the story about *Joseph and his brothers*, Genesis 37–50, is a fairytale. The opening, which is typical of this genre, is the account of the conflict between the brothers. The youngest, to whom the older brothers are ill-disposed, finally triumphs after a series of severe humiliations, and becomes the most prominent man in the state after the Pharaoh. Underlying the scene about the attempted seduction by Potiphar's wife (Gen. 39) is, as its remote proto-type, the Egyptian tale of the two brothers, which has survived in the Papyrus d'Orbiney, from the end of the Nineteenth Dynasty (1306–1186 [1295–1188] BCE) (ANET 23–25; COS 1.40; AEL 2. 203–11). Later the story of Joseph was expanded into a novella in which Joseph's vicissitudes are interpreted as an example of Yahweh's providence.

Of the original *story about Moses* only the beginning is extant, in Exodus 2–4. Moses's birth and his adoption by the Pharaoh's daughter, his flight to Midian and his marriage into the priesthood there, show the story's interest in the outstanding priestly figure who, at least according to the literary tradition, is associated with Israel's beginnings. The source breaks off with Moses's return to Egypt. Later the story about the burning bush, Exodus 3, has been interpolated. It is a cult-foundation saga, which serves as setting for the announcement of the exodus from Egypt.

The last major section of the historical work describes the *exodus of the Israelites* from Egypt and their *wanderings through the desert*. The path begins in Rameses (Exod. 12:37) and leads as far as Kadesh, on the southern entrance to Judah (Num. 20:1). Along this thread a series of episodes has been strung depicting the living conditions of the group of wanderers in the desert. Moses was not originally associated with the wilderness tradition, but he has now been added, in the scene about the *mountain of God* in the Sinai desert (Exod. 19:2–3a; 24:18b), which in the course of the literary development has become the crystallization point of the *Sinai pericope*, the great block which extends from Exodus 19 to Numbers 10, and which contains the main complex of the Old Testament law in the form of God's address to Moses. The *miracle at the Sea*, Exodus 14–15, in which Moses has the key role, was not originally part of the wilderness tradition either. That is already clear from the irreconcilability of the geographical settings.

The historical work breaks off with the story about Balaam, the seer from Transjordan, who was paid by the Moabite king Balak to curse Israel but who blesses it instead (Num. 22–24). The story reflects the disputes between Moab and the Northern Kingdom and therefore dates from the period of the monarchy. A Balaam tradition in Aramaic, dating from the eighth-seventh century BCE, was found in 1967 in Tel Deir 'Alla, in the Jordan valley (COS 2.27). From Numbers 25 onwards all traces of the Yahwist's redaction cease. Some scholars have suspected that Judges 1 contains the Yahwist version of the entry into the land of Canaan; but this is a late text, secondary to the description in the book of Joshua. It could therefore well be that the end of the work has been lost.

What the redaction intended can be seen from the sources selected. After the primeval history, which outlines the framework of the world as a whole, all the essential happenings, with one exception, take place outside Israel and Judah, which means outside the god Yahweh's given sphere of influence. The dramatis personae are all portrayed as foreigners: Hagar in the desert (Gen. 16); Lot in Sodom (Gen. 19); Abraham's servant in Mesopotamia (Gen. 24); Isaac in the country of the Philistines (Gen. 26); Jacob with Laban in Haran (Gen. 29–35); Joseph in Egypt (Gen. 39–50); also in Egypt, later, Jacob himself and his sons, the ancestors of the Israelites (Gen. 56–50); Moses in Midian (Exod. 2); the Israelites on the move in the desert, and later in Transjordan (Exod. 12–Num. 24). That this is the rule can be learnt from the exception: for the purposes of the stories about Abraham, which are set in the Israelite mountains (Gen. 12–13; 18), the editor has declared the country to be a foreign land, using the device of an artificial distinction between Israelites and Canaanites: "At that time the Canaanites were in the land" (Gen. 12:6). Taken together with the following promise, "To your descendants I will give this land" (Gen. 12:7), this makes it clear that for Abraham, Israel's settlement of the land still lay in the future. According to the fiction here, he, too, lived in the foreign country.

The Yahwist's work narrates a history of *people living in exile*. It begins with the expulsion from paradise (Gen. 3) and ends before the gates of the promised land. The path into exile is a hard fate, but it can also be a divine charge: "Go from your country" (Gen. 12:1); and for Abraham and his descendants it is linked with the promise of support and blessing (Gen. 12:2–3). Without this support things would go badly for them. Lot experiences the people of Sodom as a horde of unbridled evildoers, who surround his house and then threaten first his guests and then himself in the most brutal terms (Gen. 19). Isaac is afraid that he will be murdered by the Philistines for the sake of his wife, who is a desirable beauty (Gen. 26). Joseph is thrown into prison because of a false accusation by the Egyptian woman (Gen. 39). The Pharaoh orders the systematic annihilation of the Israelites through forced labor. When this comes to nothing, he commands the midwives to kill the Hebrews' newborn sons (Exod. 1).

In these scenes, each of which is highlighted by the redaction, we can already see the conditions in which the Jewish community lived, scattered as they were throughout the world. These conditions are also reflected in values and patterns of living. The less the individual feels himself to be in harmony with the great majority, the more important family and kinship become. Intermarriage with the indigenous population is forbidden and segregation is observed with extreme strictness (Gen. 24). Internal disputes are composed with a reminder of the special bond holding the people together (Gen. 13; 33; 37). Great importance is attached to the succession of the generations. In order to bring this out, the natural sequence of marriage, begetting, and birth is disturbed with unnatural regularity.

Sarah, Rebecca, and Rachel are all initially barren, until an heir is born through Yahweh's intervention. In this way the mere continuance of the family itself counts as a proof of Yahweh's powerfully efficacious support.

With the announcement of Isaac's birth (Gen. 18:10), the redaction, here as in many other places, employs the scheme of announcement and fulfillment. The editor does not merely describe events as such. Important happenings are regularly preceded by a promise—or a threat directed against the enemy (cf., among other passages, Gen. 12:1–3, 7; 26:3; 28:13–15; 31:3; Exod. 3:7–8; as well as Gen. 6:5–7; 18:20–21). The span of time between the announcement and the event gives the account its tension. The Yahwist's work aims to awaken hope, and its purpose is faith. The reader is supposed to see his own life embedded in the expectation of Yahweh's acts and support.

Yahweh has cast off his ties with the land of Israel and Judah and has become God of the whole world, the "God of heaven" (Gen. 24:3, 7). The relation to him is no longer mediated through the place where this God has his sphere of influence. It is the clan's worship of Yahweh as such which establishes the relationship. God becomes "the God of the Fathers," for whom, as Albrecht Alt puts it, "it is no longer the firm ties with a particular place but the permanent relationship to a group of people which is the essential characteristic." Wherever his adherents happen to be, he demonstrates his efficacy, which is full of blessing: "I am with you and will keep you wherever you go, and will bring you back to this land." To this promise

Jacob answers, astonished, "Surely Yahweh is in this place, and I did not know it" (Gen. 28:1–16). The scene takes place in Bethel, the sanctuary of what formerly had been the Northern Kingdom, and therefore also signifies the objection to Jerusalem's claim to be the only legitimate shrine for the Yahweh cult. For life in the Diaspora, it was essential to do away with the restriction to the central sanctuary.

For all that, however, Yahweh is still bound to the confines of his origin. The redaction claims him for its own interests without any reservation. From beginning to end, there is a cleft between the people who belong to Yahweh and the vast majority who are far from him. The extreme case is the Flood: only Noah survives, together with his family. All the rest are destroyed. This pattern is repeated in the downfall of Sodom (Gen. 19) and the destruction of the Egyptians in the Sea (Exod. 14), where in both cases it means the deliverance of the oppressed minority from the hostile local majority.

The Yahwist's history is the oldest history of Judaism's origins. On the other hand it has not unjustly been viewed as the "Israelite national epic." The redaction could claim to have presented the tradition which was essential for the self-understanding of Yahweh's people. The language and the world of ideas are courtly in origin. Whereas the stories about the patriarchs were originally set in a clan milieu, it is courtly language which prevails in the dialogues which the redaction has added. The epiphanies follow the pattern of the royal cult, and the theological concepts resemble those of the earlier psalms. The redaction is thoroughly familiar with the formal language used in legal proceedings. It has a Wisdom touch, and uses virtuoso didactic methods.

If we put the two things together—the experience of exile and affiliation to the Judean court—it would seem clear that we have to look for the redactor in the circle round King Jehoiachin, who was carried off into Babylonian exile in 597. The Yahwist's history is probably the earliest testimony of the Babylonian Jewish community.

THE DEUTERONOMISTIC HISTORY

On the other hand, the Deuteronomistic history originated in the land of Judah, and openly supports the traditional Yahweh religion of the Davidic kings. The problem for which the work seeks a solution springs from a fundamentally restorative political stance: Nebuchadnezzar had destroyed the Judean monarchy in Jerusalem; but without a king belonging to David's line, an independent rule had always seemed inconceivable. The problem became acute because in the second third of the sixth century BCE the Neo-Babylonian empire began to decline rapidly. This encouraged Judean expectations. It is in this situation that the redaction, drawing on the sources that had been preserved, writes the history of the Israelite and Judean kings. It puts forward evidence for the monarchy's divinely willed necessity and describes its errors as well as its times of glory, in order to acquire theological and political guidelines for the future.

The rise of Persia to the status of a world power proved that the hope of restoration was illusory. With Cambyses' Egyptian campaign of 525 BCE, Persia arrived on the Palestinian political scene. Under Darius I (522–486 BCE), Judah was incorporated into the Persian satrapy Trans-Euphrates, and the rebuilding of the temple was put in hand (520–515 BCE)—but by the Persian overlord, not the Davidic king. The original historical work did not as yet know about this development. The difficulty was surmounted by replacing hope for the monarchy by the ideal of the direct kingship of God. That prompted a series of literary revisions, which subjected history retrospectively to the conditions of the post-state theocracy. From now on the introduction of the human king was accounted a sin which had been doomed to fail, and indeed had even been the cause of the downfall. These revisions were detected and distinguished from the profile of the earlier redaction only recently.

The point at which the Deuteronomistic History begins, in the literary sense, is uncertain. For a long time it was viewed as beginning with Deuteronomy, but it has emerged that the historical recapitulation in Deuteronomy 1–3 is not an independent beginning. It presupposes considerable parts of the preceding book of Numbers. We can no longer exclude the possibility that the beginning of the Deuteronomistic work has been lost.

In the book of Judges and the books of Samuel the account rests on ancient narrative cycles, and in the books of Kings on the annals of the court and the temple (see pages 38–40). The sources show that underlying the sequence of the individual books as we have it today there is in fact a unified work: the separation of the books of Judges and Samuel, as well as the separation of the books of Samuel and Kings, cuts up in each case what was before the redaction a unified collection. Since the books of Joshua and Judges were also separated at a later point, as the double mention of Joshua's death shows (Josh. 24:29–31//Judg. 2:7–9), and since the beginning of the book of Joshua points back to the death of Moses reported in Deuteronomy 34, the original redactional concept must already have covered the course of history from the pre-state period until the downfall of Jerusalem.

As is only to be expected, the account is biased. The redaction has selected its sources rigorously, and occasionally even mutilated them. The editorial hand can best be seen from the regular assessment of the Israelites in the book of Judges, and of the kings of Israel and Judah in the books of Kings: "He did what was evil/right in Yahweh's eyes." The judgment is in most cases elaborated further, and in this way shows the yardstick which is being applied.

The kings of Israel are condemned wholesale. The reason is that "they walked in the way of Jeroboam, the son of Nebat, who made Israel sin." The formulation points back to the account which tells how Jeroboam I, the first king of the Northern Kingdom after it had separated from the Davidic dynasty, established two sanctuaries in Bethel and Dan, as rivals to the temple in Jerusalem (1 Kings 12:26–30): "And this thing became a sin." Politically, it is obvious that the division of the monarchies also affected the cult. But this is energetically denied by the redaction, for which only the temple in Jerusalem is Yahweh's legitimate sanctuary. That is quite simply Deuteronomy's cultic-political program (see page 43). It is because of this casting back to Deuteronomy that the history has been given the name of *Deuteronomistic* History. The same yardstick is applied to the kings of Judah, in a different way. With the exception of Hezekiah and Josiah, they had tolerated the local shrines ("the high places").

However, the determination of the site of the cult was not the only norm: the Judean kings Asa, Jehoshaphat, Joash, Amaziah, Asariah, and Jotham are given good marks, even though they did not intervene against "the high places." On the other hand, the kings Omri and Ahab in the Northern Kingdom, and Manasseh in the Southern Kingdom, are judged severely. They did not only contravene the cultic order; they were unfaithful to Yahweh himself. The redaction accuses Ahab of having introduced the cult of Baal (1 Kings 16:30–31) and laid the cult of the stars at Manasseh's door (2 Kings 21:3). Because, according to 2 Kings 10, Jehu had eradicated the Baal from Israel, he is the only king of the Northern Kingdom who is not explicitly condemned, although he, too, clung to the sin of Jeroboam (2 Kings 10:28–29).

Hezekiah (2 Kings 18:3–4) and Josiah (2 Kings 22:2; 23:25) are given an entirely positive assessment. David, the founder of the dynasty, counts as the yardstick (1 Kings 15:3, 11; 2 Kings 14:3; 16:2; 18:3; 22:2). For the redaction, Josiah especially, the last successful king of Judah, embodies the ideal. It was he who concentrated the Yahweh cult in Jerusalem (2 Kings 23:8). Under Josiah the Deuteronomic law, which Josiah himself probably promulgated, became reality, politically and in the cult. With this measure Josiah claimed the sovereignty of the Davidic kings over the (former) Northern Kingdom. It would seem obvious that he used the decline of Assyria in the seventh century BCE to recover control over parts of Israel which had once been possessed by David and Solomon. A Greater Judah under the name of *Israel* is also the program of the Deuteronomistic History. One way in which the redaction brings this out is continually to relate the reigns of the kings of Israel and Judah to each other, thus presenting the history of the two states as a dual unity.

In the country which had been robbed of its monarchy and was under alien rule, the remembrance of Josiah became the blueprint for the future. The circumstances of the postmonarchical present were depicted as premonarchical. This is shown by the fact that the historical work lets a premonarchical era of unsettled conditions of rule, in which disorder and misery increasingly spread, antecede the era of the kings, so that the disorder may finally be surmounted by the monarchy under Saul and David, which was both willed and inaugurated by Yahweh. The redaction built up this historical fiction by fusing into a composition the stories collected in the present book of Judges, using a framework to give them a historical sequence which follows a particular rhythm. At the beginning the leader dies. Deprived of their ruling authority, the Israelites "do what is evil in the sight of

Yahweh." They are unfaithful to Yahweh. As a result they are defeated by their enemies. In their affliction they cry to Yahweh. Called upon as advocate, Yahweh sends them a "deliverer," who vanquishes their enemies and brings about peace—for the term of forty or even eighty years. When the deliverer dies the same pattern is repeated.

The deliverers have the same function as the kings: they "judge" (that is, rule) Israel. For considerable periods of time they also succeed one another in office. Their rule is dated. They are buried like kings. The succession is emphasized in that the redaction incorporates into the sequence of the stories two straight lists of office-holders (Judges 10:1–5; 12:8–15). In fact the premonarchical leaders differ from the kings only because they do not found dynasties. But the deficiency is compensated for by quantity: Gideon had 70 sons (Judges 8:30), Jair 30 sons on 30 asses (Judges 10:4), Ibzan 30 sons, 30 daughters, and 30 daughters-in-law (Judges 12:9), Abdon 4 sons and 30 grandsons who rode 70 asses (Judges 12:14). The ass as mount is an attribute of kings.

Towards the end of the epoch the succession of office-holders breaks off. The deliverer Samson (Judges 13–16) is in office for only half the forty years during which the Philistines oppress Israel. Peace does not return again. "In those days there was no king in Israel; every man did what was right in his own eyes" (Judges 17:6)—not what was right in the eyes of Yahweh. As in the books of Kings, the king—or, in fact, the lack of one—is of essential importance for Israel's relationship to God. Everything comes down to the people's urgent request to Samuel: "Appoint for us a king to govern us like all the nations" (1 Sam. 8:5). The request is in line with the Deuteronomic commandment (Deut. 17:14–20) and is fulfilled by Yahweh with the anointing of Saul.

The monarchy reaches its climax under David and Solomon. "Judah and Israel dwelt in safety, from Dan even to Beer-sheba, every man under his vine and under his fig tree, all the days of Solomon" (1 Kings 4:25). From this point a light is shed on the end of the Deuteronomistic History in 2 Kings 25:27–30. It reports that when Amel-Marduk, Nebuchadnezzar's successor, came to the throne (562 BCE), Jehoiachin, the last survivor of the Davidic kings, was released. It is true that the note reads as if Jehoiachin was already dead when the redactor was writing. But nevertheless his release was evidently seen as a sign of the return of the Davidic dynasty.

From beginning to end, therefore, the Deuteronomistic History presents the proof that from early times it had been Yahweh's purpose to establish David's kingdom and the temple in Jerusalem: they were the outcome of his will and election. The continuance of the dynasty was therefore guaranteed. For the very reason that the temple was in ruins and required a builder from David's line, Yahweh was bound to give a new turn to events.

THE BEGINNINGS
OF OLD TESTAMENT THEOLOGY

The Book of Jeremiah

Hopes for the return of the Judean monarchy foundered on the Persians. With this it became clear that the downfall of Jerusalem had meant the end of the traditional Yahweh religion. Towards the end of the sixth century BCE it became inescapably necessary to face up to the consequences of the catastrophe. The interpretation was elicited from the prophecy that had been handed down.

Jeremiah, the last of the prophets of pre-exilic Judah, was the most important. His sayings and symbolic actions, as well as the accounts of his fate at the court in Jerusalem, formed the basis for a comprehensive rethinking. In retrospect, Jeremiah's lament over the catastrophe that was impending could be read as prophetic prediction. Understood in this sense, it offered the possibility of interpreting the downfall as Yahweh's act, his divine judgment. From this the indictment of the Judeans emerged: they had been punished by Yahweh because they had turned away from him. But this also made it possible to arrive at guidelines for the future, whether as a demand for repentance and new obedience, or whether as Yahweh's promise to restore conditions as they had once been.

The outcome was Old Testament *covenant theology*. This gave the traditional dynastic and national religion a new, conscious form. What had been, as it were, a "natural" Yahweh religion was replaced by the deliberate decision for the god Yahweh, a decision which had continually to be repeated afresh. It was a faith which had to prove itself in conscious obedience to God's commands, and which had to be justified to oneself and to others. The book of Jeremiah reflects the beginnings of this development, which was decisive for all that was to come. This theology is generally called "Deuteronomistic," and it is true that it is found in particularly pronounced form in Deuteronomy. Nonetheless, however, it originates not in the law but in prophecy.

At the beginning was *the breach between Yahweh and his people*. Sayings such as "The end has come upon my people Israel" (Amos 8:2), or "You are not my people and I am not your God" (Hosea 1:9), which had once been directed against the hostile Northern Kingdom (see page 56f.), now took on a different coloring. We can see this happening from the recurrence of Amos's vision in Jer. 1:11–14. The book of Jeremiah includes other, comparable utterances. They have been handed down as interpretative oracles, in the scenic framework of symbolic actions.

> Behold, I will make to cease . . . before your eyes and
> in your days the voice of mirth and the voice of

gladness, the voice of the bridegroom and the voice of the bride. (Jer. 16:9)

Behold, like the clay in the potter's hand, so are you in my hand. (Jer. 18:6)

So will I break this people . . . as one breaks a potter's vessel, so that it can never be mended. (Jer. 19:11)

These symbolic actions (Jer. 13; 16; 18; 19; 29; 32; 35; 36) form an appendix to the nucleus of the book: the poems about the enemy from the north (Jer. 4–6; 8–9; and also scattered throughout Jer. 10–23 and 30–31; see page 59). Like the books of Amos, Hosea, and Isaiah, the book of Jeremiah in its earliest form combines a collection of prophetic sayings with symbolic actions and/or visions. The earliest form of the book is introduced by the call scene in Jeremiah 1, a copy of the call of Isaiah in Isaiah 6. The leading theme of this introduction, which is also a leitmotif in the symbolic actions, is the *Word of Yahweh*. Historical experience has proved the truth of the prophetic proclamation; this proclamation is now theologically conceptualized.

This earliest book of Jeremiah formed the "text" of a continuing interpretation in which new attempts were again and again made to come to terms with Israel's exilic fate. Excursuses comprising a theology of history were interpolated in the form of great *divine addresses* to the prophet (e.g., Jer. 7; 11; 19; 32; 44). They are distinguished from the earlier material in being prose, no longer poetry. The style is so striking that these texts have occasionally been attributed to a separate source, or to a redaction working according to a particular plan. Justification of the judgment in the form of question and answer characterizes the pattern of the argumentation.

> When you tell this people all these words, and they say to you, "Why has Yahweh pronounced all this great evil against us? What is our iniquity? What is the sin that we have committed against Yahweh our God?" then you shall say to them: "Because your fathers have forsaken me, says Yahweh, and have gone after other gods and have served and worshipped them, . . . and because you have done worse than your fathers; for behold, every one of you follows his stubborn evil will, refusing to listen to me." (Jer. 16:10–11a,12; cf. Jer. 5:19; 9:11–15; 22:8–9; Deut. 29:23–27; 1 Kings 9:8–9)

The "why" question, which determined the exilic and postexilic period, is so tormenting because it already presupposes that Yahweh did not just announce the disaster; he also brought it about. Consequently Judah's catastrophe counts not as the god Yahweh's defeat, but as his punitive action against his own people. The reason must surely have been Israel's disobedience: "What is our iniquity?" The answer strikes at the roots of religion: the fathers turned to other gods, and the present generation is doing the same. Just because the reproach is nonsense, in the sense of the history of religion, it characterizes the change which had come about at the end of the sixth century BCE; for right until the end, the population of pre-exilic Judah had no reason to turn their backs on their dynastic god Yahweh. In extreme crises one does not throw one's religious identity over board. It was only when the Judean monarchy had been destroyed and the Temple lay in ruins that the "other gods" became an alternative. From now on, the First Commandment, "You shall have no other gods before me" (Exod. 20:3) is the foundation of the Old Testament faith. The manifold results can be found in the rest of the book of Jeremiah, as well as in Deuteronomy, in the book of Ezekiel, and in the Priestly source.

On this newly acquired foundation, the present is addressed as if the downfall were still impending. This is especially true of the great Temple speech:

> Thus says Yahweh, the God of Israel, Amend your ways and your doings, and I will dwell beside you in this place. Do not trust in these deceptive words: "This is Yahweh's temple, this is Yahweh's temple, this is Yahweh's temple!" . . . Is it not so: you steal, murder, commit adultery, swear falsely, burn incense to Baal, and go after other gods that you have not known, and then come and stand before me in this house, which is called by my name, and say, We are safe! (Jer. 7:3–4, 9–10a)

The presence of the Deity in the national sanctuary is no longer a matter of course. Yahweh makes his protective and solicitous presence dependent on whether or not the Judeans remain faithful to him. And here, all of a sudden, ethics comes into competition with the cult. Implicit here is also an answer to the question which the accusation was bound to evoke among the Judeans: So what should we do? The admonition, however, is linked with the promise: "If you obey I will dwell beside you in this place." The return to Yahweh is not without its reward. A new beginning is possible.

The weight given to such promises is especially great in the book of Jeremiah. The two oldest promises may even derive from the prophet himself: the saying about buying fields, and the letter to the people in Babylonian exile. Both have been handed down in the framework of symbolic actions.

> Houses and fields and vineyards shall again be bought in this land. (Jer. 32:15)

> Build houses and live in them; plant gardens and eat their produce. Take wives . . . and multiply there, and do not decrease. Seek the welfare of the city . . . and pray to Yahweh on its behalf, for in its welfare you will find your welfare. (Jer. 29:5–7)

Building and planting, the acquisition of houses, fields, and vineyards mean the return to normal commercial and family life after the catastrophe. At the same time, the letter to the people in exile is ambivalent. It does not hold out the prospect of an end to the exile. Instead it advises the people to view existence in the foreign land as a longstanding state of affairs: this is salvation in judgment.

With increasing distance from the catastrophe, reservations of this kind are dropped. Now we also hear the promise without any qualifications at all. The most famous of these promises touches the relationship to God itself. Yahweh promises to forgive his people of his own free will, and to re-establish the covenant that had been broken:

> Behold, the days are coming, says Yahweh, when I will make a new covenant with the house of Israel and the house of Judah, not like the covenant which I made with their fathers when I took them by the hand to bring them out of the land of Egypt, my covenant which they broke. Then I will be lord over them, says Yahweh, . . . and I will be their God, and they shall be my people. And no longer shall each man teach his neighbor and each his brother, saying, "Know Yahweh," for they shall all know me, from the least of them to the greatest, says Yahweh; for I will forgive their iniquity, and I will remember their sin no more. (Jer. 31:31–32, 33b–34).

The step taken here was inescapable: as soon as the historical catastrophe was put down to the fact that Israel had ceased to be faithful to Yahweh and had broken the covenant, the relationship to God could no longer be made to depend on the simple demand for faithfulness and obedience. A new covenant, which did not already harbor within itself the germ of renewed failure, could only be a unilateral act of forgiving love, which had its foundation and its enduring existence on God's side alone.

One reason why the book of Jeremiah has evoked so much interest is that here the prophet as *person* occupies more space than in any other of the prophetic books. Or at least this would seem to be the case. The presumption has three roots. For one thing, from early on, as an appendix to the symbolic actions, the book

already included the story of Jeremiah's imprison-
ment (Jer. 37), a story which is expanded in Jeremiah
38–44 by further accounts of the prophet's sufferings,
to the point of his deportation to Egypt. Then, in the
early postexilic period, a widespread discussion broke
out about the nature of true prophecy. We can see
why: the prophetic sayings which had been handed
down, and which the people had learnt to see as an
announcement of divine judgment, were in all too
crass a contradiction to the present longings for salvation. The dispute with the false prophets of salvation
was depicted by way of the person of Jeremiah. This
finds expression, for example, in the encounter with
the prophet Hananiah (Jer. 28). Finally, the laments
about the enemy from the North evoke the impression
in places of being prompted by personal torment (e.g.,
Jer. 20:14–18). All this made Jeremiah in later times the
epitome of the righteous man—here as prophet—who
is condemned to suffer. This picture found literary expression in the so-called confessions in Jeremiah
11:18–12:6; 15:10–12, 15–21; 17:14–18; 18:18–23; and
20:7–13.

> Yahweh, you have deceived me,
> and I was deceived.
> You are stronger than I,
> and you have prevailed.
> I have become a laughingstock all the day;
> everyone mocks me.
> For whenever I speak, I cry out,
> I shout, "Violence and destruction!" . . .
> If I say, "I will not mention him,

or speak any more in his name,"
there is in my heart as it were a burning fire
shut up in my bones,
and I am weary with holding it in,
and I cannot. (Jer. 20:7–8a, 9)

Scholars have attached particular importance to these apparently autobiographical confessions, for it seemed as if it might be possible here to detect the authentic voice of the prophet's own self-understanding. But a glance at the late psalms shows that in these texts it is the devout, exposed to the hostility of others, who have identified themselves with the prophet and his lot. The prayers are not the prophet's confessions; they are an interpretation of his fate and his message.

In this way the book of Jeremiah continued to grow, down to the latest period. In spite of occasional attempts to give it shape, it never attained a final form. The borders remained fluid. The outward sign of this is the different compass of the Greek text, which is shorter than the Hebrew by an eighth.

CHAPTER 7

❧

THE THEOLOGICAL SIGNIFICANCE OF THE LAW

As soon as the relationship to God ceases to be a matter of course, but depends, as a conscious attitude, on a decision which has continually to be re-endorsed, it requires standards against which it can test itself. The response to God's commitment and promise therefore takes place in obedience to God's instruction (Heb.: *tôrāh*). Knowledge of this Torah, and the concurrence of personal existence and actions with the Torah, became the central substance of the Jewish faith.

The source of this instruction was first of all prophecy; for it was the prophets who had authoritatively communicated the will of God in the given situation. The laws that had been handed down, on the other hand, ordered social life. Even if the law did not exist without the religious dimension—law without religion would have been inconceivable in antiquity—its norms were not divine law in the direct sense. The relationship to God itself required no law. Consequently, seen in the narrowest sense as religious practice, the Old Testament law is later than the prophets. The origins of the Torah belong to the beginning of the postexilic period.

There were two ways of codifying God's will: a new divine law could be drawn up on the basis of the prophetic proclamation; and the existing law could be annotated from the standpoint of the relationship to God. Both of these ways were followed, at about the same time. The outcome of the first is the *Decalogue*; the outcome of the second is *Deuteronomy*, worked over from the perspective of covenant theology.

THE DECALOGUE

The "Ten Commandments" are the quintessence of Old Testament law. They originate as the translation of prophetic admonition into authoritative divine law.

The series of commandments familiar to us alternates between commands and prohibitions, between what Yahweh says, and what is said about Yahweh. It comprises short and long instructions, some furnished with a reason and some without. The inconsistencies show that a distinction has to be made between the seminal stratum and later expansions. In its basic form, the series may have been as follows:

> I am Yahweh your God, who brought you out of the land of Egypt, out of the house of bondage. You shall have no other gods before me. . . . Do not bow down to them and do not worship them. . . . You shall not murder. You shall not commit adultery. You shall not steal. You shall not bear false witness against your neighbor. You shall not covet your neighbor's house. (Exod. 20:2–3, 5a, 13–17a)

It is not difficult to recognize in this compilation the catalogue of iniquities in Jeremiah's Temple speech:

> Steal, murder, commit adultery, swear falsely, burn incense to Baal, and go after other gods that you have not known! (Jer. 7:9)

This sweeping polemic, which can be found again in very similar form in Hosea 4:2 (see page 131), is now transformed into a list of ethical norms. The prophetic proclamation of God's will has crystallized into a series of commandments. The roots in polemic are still evident; for even if the Decalogue sums up in masterly fashion the fundamental requirements of a religiously based ethics, it does not rest on a system of law. Apart from the arrangement of the themes, this is also shown by the details: the Hebrew verb *rṣḥ*, which is used for the injunction against intentional killing, is used elsewhere for unintentional manslaughter (Num. 35; Deut. 19:1–7; Josh. 20). But apart from these shortcomings, here the step to the divine Old Testament law has been effectively taken.

The Decalogue is distinguished from prophetic polemic by its style and atmosphere. The beginning, with the self-introduction "I am Yahweh," is derived from the cult. It shows that the series of commandments is a revelatory speech (see page 48). As is often the case, the name of God is not left on its own but is expanded by attributes emphasizing both his help and his claim. Yahweh points to his foundational saving act: he had brought Israel out of Egypt. With this act of deliverance he established his relationship to Israel. It is this act that provides the basis for the demand: "You shall have no other gods before me. You shall not bow down to them or serve them." Israels's exclusive relationship to God, as the focus of the series of commandments, is moved to the beginning. It is the first of all commandments. The ethical directives are consequences. In these, Israel maintains its relationship to its God, and precisely by doing so preserves the freedom that has been conferred on it.

The series in its basic form was later expanded. The other commandments are no longer derived from prophecy, but, as we might expect, have been extracted from the wealth of other laws for the purpose of this basic law. Three of them add important features to the First Commandment especially: the injunction against misusing the name of God (in taking an oath, from Exodus 23:1); the prohibition of idols (from Exodus 34:17, prompted by the story about the Golden Calf in Exodus 32); and the commandment about the sabbath rest (from Exodus 34:21). All three have put a profound stamp on Jewish faith. It was obedience to these three commandments which gave practical form to the First Commandment.

The beginning of stagecraft is already evident in Yahweh's self-introduction. It was interpolated into the traditional story about God in such a way that it also links up with the liberation from Egypt. After the passage through the sea, and in the framework of Yahweh's appearance on the Mountain of God in the Sinai desert, Moses receives the commandments

(Exod. 20). After he has come down from the mountain, he commits the people to their observance:

> Moses came and told the people all the words
> of Yahweh . . . ; and all the people answered with
> one voice, and said, "All the words which Yahweh
> has spoken we will do." (Exod. 24:3*)

With this commitment the Decalogue becomes "the Book of the Covenant" (Exod. 24:7), the law of God per se.

As far as the composition of the Pentateuch is concerned, the result was that, following on the Decalogue, the mass of Old Testament laws was gradually added. In the light of the covenant between Yahweh and Israel, these laws now all purport to be read as Yahweh's Torah. They include the Book of the Covenant (see page 42), the laws about the sanctuary, the priesthood and sacrifice, taken from the Priestly source (see page 101), the series of commandments in Exodus 34 (which used often to be seen as an ancient "cultic" Decalogue, but which is in fact a secondary conglomerate), and "the Holiness Code," Leviticus 17–26 (a body of law which belongs historically between Deuteronomy and the Priestly source). Through these expansions, the scene on the Mountain of God in Sinai has therefore been much extended, reaching from Exodus 19 to Numbers 10, and the course of events during the wanderings in the wilderness has been thrown out of balance. The theological systemization was more important than the consistent progress of the story.

DEUTERONOMY

Deuteronomy is the only law which did not find its way into the Sinaitic enactments. The reason was very probably that this body of law already had a fixed place beforehand in the course of salvation history: Moses proclaims it to the Israelites in Transjordan immediately before the passage through the Jordan. In spite of its actual origin in the seventh century BCE, in its biblical context it counts as the religious and ethical norm dating from the early period: it was according to this norm that God's people were supposed to order their lives after they had reached the Promised Land.

The original form of this norm as it can be elicited from the body of Deuteronomy 12–26 (see page 43), still antecedes the qualitative leap which is signified by the emergence of the theological law. Today, however, Deuteronomy also counts as divine law. It is even the first great complex of law in the Old Testament which has itself become the object of the relationship to God. For, unlike the Decalogue, this is not a new series of commandments emerging from the idea of the covenant; it is rather that already existing law was retrospectively moved into the conditioning context of the covenant with God.

At first sight, it would seem as if it was again the Decalogue which provided the means for this; for we find the Decalogue a second time in Deuteronomy 5, so that it also introduces the Deuteronomic law. By way of this structure, Deuteronomy is related to the Decalogue in such a way that it seems to provide the individual instructions for the basic articles. But in fact the repetition is merely a late doublet of Exodus 20, which is intended to put Deuteronomy on the same level as the Sinaitic laws. It does not bring us to the heart of the matter.

The real covenant-theology clothing is supplied rather by the prelude in Deuteronomy 6–11, which has not without reason been called "the chief commandment." It begins with the finest expression of the conscious relationship to God which can be found in the Old Testament, the "love" commandment of the *Sch^{e}ma'*:

> Hear, O Israel: Yahweh is our God, Yahweh is one; and you shall love Yahweh your God with all your heart, and with all your soul, and with all your might. (Deut. 6:4–5)

The change from the singular form of address, "Hear, O Israel," to the acknowledgment in the "we" form, "Yahweh is our God," shows that the commandment was not originally a single unit. An already existing creed has been taken up and set in a new context. It may perhaps date from the time when, after the downfall of the Northern Kingdom, the surviving Judah set about appropriating the Yahweh tradition of the brother kingdom with which, at the end, it had stood in bitter conflict. It did so by emphasizing that Yahweh, who, as we know from nonbiblical texts, was also worshipped as, among other things, "Yahweh of Samaria" and "Yahweh of Teman" (COS 2.46 A–C), was to be understood as a *single* Yahweh.

An addition in the singular form of address states that Israel's relationship to God, which is the subject of the creed "Yahweh is our God," becomes effective in the love of God which interpenetrates the whole of existence. "Love" does not mean an emotion; it means loyalty and obedience—in fact, that which the First Commandment in the Decalogue describes in the form of the prohibition, "You shall have no other gods before me." This commandment of love is far removed from a casuistic legalism. Judaism has rightly discerned that this commandment is the summing up of the Torah, and in this respect Christianity has followed Judaism (Mark 12:28–34).

The *Sch^ema'* was once the opening of the prelude, and it is also the most important statement: it is the oldest theological interpretation, in the narrower sense, of the Deuteronomic law. What follows in Deuteronomy 6–11 is related to it as variations on the given theme. The following verse seems already to lead over to the main block, Deuteronomy 12–26: "And these words which I command you this day shall be upon your heart" (Deut. 6:6). It is only the later explanatory expositions in verses 7–9, which, as they stand, can be applied only to the *Sch^ema'* itself (and today shape the daily Jewish prayer ritual) that blur the direct relation to the main body of the law. Under the heading of the *Sch^ema'*, the Deuteronomic law can be read as a summing-up of what it means in specific cases to love Yahweh with all one's heart, and with all one's soul, and with all one's might.

The first and oldest sentence of the concluding framework is related to the opening frame like a closing bracket:

> This day Yahweh your God commands you to do
> these statutes and ordinances; you shall therefore

be careful to do them with all your heart and with
all your soul. (Deut. 26:16)

In Deuteronomy 6:4–6 and 26:16 we find the origin of
the insistent, emotionally appealing exhortation to un-
divided obedience which today appears as the special
character of Deuteronomy.

A little later, a covenant formula is added to the
concluding framework. Through this the law also becomes the very substance of the covenant with God.

> You have declared this day concerning Yahweh that
> he is your God, and that you will walk in his ways,
> and keep his statutes and his commandments
> and his ordinances, and will obey his voice; and
> Yahweh has declared this day concerning you that
> you are a people for his own possession, as he has
> promised you, and that you are to keep all his
> commandments. (Deut. 26:17–18)

The scene is apparently meant to record a mutual dec-
laration, but it can only do so in makeshift form, because Deuteronomy as a whole is clothed in the
language and style of Moses's address. In content, too,
the two sides have not been given equal weight.
Israel's obligation to keep the covenant is a response
to Yahweh's promise of that covenant. Theologically
speaking, this is the only possible sequence.

The later framing provided by the commandment
for love and the covenant obligation changes the
genre of the whole complex: what was earlier a law
book becomes a kind of contract between a vassal and
the deity. There were political models for this. One is

the oath of loyalty which the kings were accustomed to require of their officials; another—though more remote—was the contracts between great kings and the vassal-kings who were subject to their authority. The application of a treaty of loyalty like this to the direct relationship between deity and people necessarily presupposes the end of the monarchy in Judah. Deuteronomy as a loyalty treaty conforms neither to the pattern of an already concluded covenant, nor to its repetition in worship; it follows solely the inner logic of the theological issue.

A loyalty pact includes the threat of sanctions should the contract be broken. Consequently Deuteronomy now ends with the announcement of blessing and curse.

> If you obey the voice of Yahweh your God, being careful to do all his commandments which I command you this day, . . . all these blessings shall come upon you and overtake you. . . . Blessed shall you be in the city, and blessed shall you be in the field. Blessed shall be the fruit of your body, and the fruit of your ground, and the fruit of your beasts, the increase of your cattle, and the young of your flock. Blessed shall be your basket and your kneading-trough. Blessed shall you be when you come in, and blessed shall you be when you go out.
>
> But if you will not obey the voice of Yahweh your God or be careful to do all his commandments and his statutes which I command you this day, then all these curses shall come upon you and overtake you. Cursed shall you be in the city, and cursed shall you

be in the field. Cursed shall be your basket and your
kneading-trough. Cursed shall be the fruit of your
body, and the fruit of your ground, the increase of
your cattle, and the young of your flock. Cursed
shall you be when you come in, and cursed shall
you be when you go out. (Deut. 28:1a, 2a, 3–6, 15–19).

In today's text, the original core of this passage has
grown into one of the longest and cruellest curses in
the literature of the world. The terrible experiences of
suffering and downfall which the Judeans had under-
gone under the Neo-Babylonians provide the examples, and the threatening oracles of the prophets
provide the text. From now on it is obedience to the
law which becomes the expression of the relationship
to God.

A multiplicity of other commandments has then
been interpolated into this framework. For the most
part, Deuteronomy acquired its ethical profundity only
later. Today it reads like the program for life in the community of Yahweh. There are no signs that a state order
existed, except for local jurisdiction. The social and ethical features of this communal order, for which broth-
erly love is paramount, have somewhat of an utopian
character. That contributed rather to the programmatic
influence, an influence which was immense, both
within the Old Testament and outside of it.

CHAPTER 8

❀

THE STRUGGLE FOR PRECEDENCE BETWEEN THE THEOLOGIANS FROM THE EXILE AND THE JERUSALEM TEMPLE SCHOOL

The Book of Ezekiel

After the court of Jehoiachin had been deported in 597 BCE, there came to be a second spiritual center in Babylon for the emerging Jewish community. Since the Davidic dynasty initially continued to exist in exile, while in Jerusalem it had been snuffed out in 586 BCE, those in Babylon felt especially called to spiritual leadership. That led to conflicts as soon as—from the fifth century BCE onwards—groups of Babylonian Jews began to return to Jerusalem. The question was, who was authorized to lay down the standards for the formation of the theological system? The Babylonian Jews were able to make their views prevail. According to the picture given to us in the Bible, the continuity of God's people was sustained exclusively via the Exile. For seventy years the country of Judah was supposed to be a wasteland, stripped of its inhabitants. It was only the return from Babylon which, we are told, made the rebuilding of the Temple possible.

Where the history of ideas is concerned, however, it was not those who returned from exile who were the victors; it was the Palestinian theologians. The texts which served as sources for the further development were the book of Jeremiah, Deuteronomy and the Deuteronomistic History—all of which originated in, or in the region of, Jerusalem. This body of texts was appropriated by the Babylonian theologians.

Their method was to gloss the book of Jeremiah in such a way that now all the prophecies of salvation concerned only the people in exile, and the returnees. The people of Jerusalem, on the other hand, are told that they will be completely blotted out "by the sword, by famine, and by pestilence" (cf. Jer. 21:1–10). After the conquest, Nebuchadnezzar was said to have deported the rest of the population so that only the "poorest people of the land" (2 Kings 24:14) were left behind—according to another reading, not even these. Finally, all those left behind, including all those who had fled into the neighboring countries, allegedly emigrated to Egypt. There Jeremiah had once more to proclaim to them that they faced complete annihilation (Jer. 44).

What became the programmatic text for the preeminence of the Babylonian Jews is the book of Ezekiel, which is attributed to a priest of that name, Ezekiel, the son of Buzi. The oldest part of the book can most probably be found in the richly imaged laments over the fate of the kings of Judah, which have been preserved in Ezekiel 19. But it emerges from the metaphorical language about the cedar and the eagle in Ezekiel 17 that the struggle for precedence

between the court in Babylon and the Davidic sup-
porters in Jerusalem came to the fore not much later.

The conflict was bound to escalate once the Babylonian Jews started to return.

> The word of Yahweh came to me: "Son of man, the
> inhabitants of these waste places in the land of
> Israel keep saying, 'Abraham was only one man,
> yet he got possession of the land; but we are many;
> the land is surely given us to possess. . . . Say this to
> them. Thus says Yahweh: As I live, surely those
> who are in the waste places shall fall by the sword;
> and him that is in the open field I will give to
> the beasts to be devoured; and those who are in
> strongholds and in caves shall die by pestilence.
> And I will make the land a desolation and a waste."
> (Ezek. 33:23–24, 27–28*)

The book was revised so as to suggest that even before
the conquest of Jerusalem Ezekiel had already proclaimed the complete downfall of the city, and the preeminence of the people who had been carried off into
exile in 597 BCE. To judge by its language, the book
presupposes the revised book of Jeremiah as well as
Deuteronomy, including its covenant-theology framework. Jeremian-Deuteronomic theology is given an individual stamp. Although, accordingly, in the context
of theological history the book of Ezekiel in fact belongs to the fifth century BCE, the dates relate to the
exile of Jehoiachin. Although the dispute took place in
Judah, Ezekiel is supposed to have preached at the
Chebar River in Babylon. But so that in spite of that
he could talk about conditions in Judah, the spirit of

Yahweh is supposed to have carried him off to Jerusalem. In the great translation vision in Ezekiel 8–11, he sees the Glory of Yahweh departing from the Temple and the city even before they have been destroyed (Ezek. 11:22–23). The Glory will return only after Temple and city have been rebuilt (Ezek. 43:1–9), a rebuilding which those who return from exile will put in hand on the model of a plan seen by Ezekiel (Ezekiel 40–42, with appendices in Ezekiel 43–48).

Later, both in the book of Jeremiah and in the book of Ezekiel, the promise to those who return is replaced by the promise to the people of the Jewish dispersion "out of all countries" that they will be gathered into the Promised Land (Jer. 16:15; 23:3, 8; 29:14; 32:37; Ezek. 34:13; 36:24). Once the rivalry between those who had remained in the country and those who had returned had been settled, the important thing was to establish Zion as the center of the worldwide Jewish community.

THE TEMPLE AS THE CENTER OF THE JEWISH DIASPORA

The Priestly Source

On the foundation of the theology of the book of Ezekiel, a new overall picture of salvation history emerged. Once again, the sequence of events from creation to the threshold of the conquest of the Promised Land was related in a great historical work. Since the end of the nineteenth century this later continuous source for the Pentateuch has been called the "Priestly source" (P). The name was given to it because it centers on the establishment of the Jerusalem Temple. It was there that the Priestly source was also most probably compiled. Since it presupposes the Ezekiel tradition, it cannot have originated before the second half of the fifth century BCE. The Priestly source is addressed to the Jewish diaspora, or dispersion, and it becomes increasingly clear in the course of the narrative that the work is adopting an outside perspective. Like the Yahwist's history, it shifts the story of the patriarchs into the foreign country, even explicitly calling Canaan "the land of your sojournings" (Gen. 17:8; 28:4; 36:7; 37:1). In a highly curious fiction, the sanctuary itself is moved into the center of the wandering people of God while they are still on their way to the land of promise.

The style of the Priestly source has been called "defining." This style appears in particularly marked form in a number of genealogies and lists, as well as sacrificial and purity laws, but it also characterizes the narratives. The Creation account, Genesis 1:1–2, 4a, is a classification of the world rather than the description of its genesis. Simply in order that the sabbath may be anchored to the beginning of the world, the whole of Creation is forced into an extremely artificial strait-jacket of six days. The ten generations between the Creation and the Flood (Gen. 5) span 1,307 years in the original text. The age of these ancestors of mankind bursts the bounds of any conceivable possibility. The record is reached with Methuselah's 969 years. In the story of the Flood, Genesis 6–9, chaos breaks in according to a precise timetable; even the water level is given. The peak of artificiality is of course that the Israelites are already given the sanctuary in the wilderness on Sinai, this sanctuary being precisely described with all its furnishings and the whole cultic personnel (Exod. 25–29; 35–40). There are frequent repetitions, and continually new nuances appear.

Many if not most of these details, however, are later additions. The source has been worked over again and again on the once-given foundation, and in P's characteristic language and world of ideas. Among the later additions are the greater part of the laws from Exodus 25 onwards; these detail the way the shrine is to be furnished, and the order and equipment of the priesthood. Appendices are the regulations about sacrifice,

Leviticus 1–6 (although earlier ordinances are taken up), and the same is true of the purity regulations, Leviticus 11–15, and the body of law known as the "Holiness Code," Leviticus 17–26, which was formerly an independent law book. In the book of Numbers, the people of God are listed according to tribes and clans, with precise numbers, on a scale which exceeds every realistic possibility (e.g., Num. 1:20–43; 26:5–62).

In order to recover the aim, without which such a fictitious outline of history would never have come into being, we have to go back to the initial form of the Priestly source. This aim emerges particularly from the way in which the material is organized. Five *structuring series* can be seen.

The most obvious is *the system of headings*, which divides up events into epochs, from Creation down to the sons of Jacob. These are the *tôlᵉdot*, (Gen. 2:4; 5:1; 6:9; 11:10, 27; 25:12, 19; 36:1; 37:2). The word *tôlᵉdot*, rendered in English as "generations," is an artificial derivative from the verb *yld*, "bear, give birth to," and means more or less "descendants"; but it is also applied to the Creation account and to narratives. Nevertheless the *genealogical* aspect is in the foreground. With Jacob and his sons, this classification, which begins with Creation, breaks off: the history of mankind which God has initiated arrives at its goal when God's people, Israel, comes into existence. In the story of the patriarchs the presentation is such that the collateral lines of this people are dealt with first: Ishmael (Gen. 25:12) before Isaac (25:19), Esau (36:1) before Jacob (37:2). These collateral lines are excluded from the history of salvation. A *topographical* scheme is linked with the genealogical one. Just as the collateral lines are excluded from the sequence of generations, they also abandon the Promised Land. This happens when Abraham and Lot separate (Gen. 13:6, 11b–12*) and is repeated in the case of Esau and Jacob (36:1, 6–8; 37:1).

The third structuring series is the *chronology*. The Priestly source offers a precise numerical series on the basis of which the course of salvation history can be dated and according to which the Jewish calendar is still calculated today. As a rule, this sequence is linked with the genealogy: we are told the age of the father when his son is born. The very artificiality shows that the time-scale must have some deeper significance. But to discover the intention is not easy. The establishment of the cult on Sinai, which follows directly on the Exodus, has been thought to be the vanishing point, the focus towards which everything draws. The span of time between Creation and the Exodus amounts to 2,666 years, according to the Masoretic text. This can be viewed as two-thirds of a world-aeon lasting 4,000 years in all.

The fourth ordering sequence has to do with *the name of God*. The Priestly source divides the history of revelation into periods in which God reveals himself with increasing clarity. In the primeval history—which is to say in the global context of mankind as a whole—the term *Elohim*, "God," is used. Yahweh reveals himself to the patriarchs, with whom the prehistory of God's people begins, under the name *'El shadday*, which is rendered in English Bibles as "God Almighty" or "the Almighty God" (Gen. 17:1; 28:3; 35:11). It is only Moses to whom *Yahweh* as the name of God is proclaimed for the first time (Exod. 6:2). There is a change of name on the human side, too: in Genesis 17 Abraham and Sarah, who are previously supposed to have been called Abram and Sarai, are given new names, and in Genesis 35 Jacob is renamed Israel, in a revelation at Bethel.

The fifth structuring series is the most important. At four decisive points in the course of the history, God gives a *covenant promise*, in direct speech: the covenant with Noah follows on the end of the Flood, which is the primal catastrophe per se (Gen. 9:9, 11*); the covenant with Abraham stands at the beginning of the story of the patriarchs, as God's special history with Israel (Gen. 17:6–8); the Exodus covenant is given when God brings the people out of Egypt, as the end of foreign rule and dispersion (Exod. 6:2–8); but the climax is reached with the giving of the covenant on Sinai, on which the command to build the sanctuary is based (Exod. 25–29*).

It is in the promise of the divine covenant that the history whose trend is implicit in all the ordering sequences arrives at its goal. The wording is taken from the book of Ezekiel:

> I will make a covenant of peace with them; it shall be an everlasting covenant with them; . . . and I will set my sanctuary in the midst of them for evermore; . . . and I will be their God, and they shall be my people. (Ezek. 37:26–27*)

This promise is endorsed by the Priestly source and its fulfilment is in part anticipated. Even if the divine history outlined here professes to have taken place in the early period, it is a reflection of the experiences and hopes of the present. The Creation, which is the beginning, offers a framework which orders the whole of existence in space and time. Order makes a successful life possible, and thus itself becomes a salutary good. But then sin breaks in and, as its consequence, chaos. In Genesis 6:13 the way in which the Flood is announced picks up the message of the prophets. God's resolve to destroy—"The end of all flesh has come before me"—goes back, by way of Ezekiel 7:2, to Amos's fourth vision: "The end has come upon my people Israel" (Amos 8:2). The reader who is versed in the biblical tradition is asked to recognize in the Flood Israel's historical catastrophes, the last of them being the conquest of Jerusalem, with its consequences for the Yahweh sanctuary and the Davidic dynasty. The first of the four covenant promises, the covenant with Noah (Gen. 9), resolutely runs counter to the downfall. It implies that God's people has its catastrophe behind it, once and for all. The preservation from the primal catastrophe is supposed to justify a kind of basic trust, which from now on determines the whole of history for all those who belong to Yahweh.

The second covenant promise is given to Abraham (Gen. 17). The Israelite who is living in the foreign country is promised that his descendants will greatly increase and will possess the land of Canaan for ever. Apparently this promise is given in the face of contrary experiences. After the promise to Jacob has been endorsed (Gen. 35:11–12), it is supplemented by the promise of liberation from slavery when the Exodus covenant is given to Moses (Exod. 6:2–8). This Exodus has a goal. That is shown by the revelation on Sinai. Its sole substance (disguised as a law about the tabernacle) is the establishment of the cult in Jerusalem, on Mount Zion.

> Yahweh said to Moses, "Speak to the people of Israel, that they take for me an offering. . . . And let them make me a sanctuary, that I may dwell in their midst. . . . I will consecrate the tent of meeting and the altar; . . . and I will dwell among the people of Israel, and will be their God. And they shall know that I am Yahweh their God, who brought them forth out of the land of Egypt that I might dwell among them; I am Yahweh, their God." (Exod. 25:1–2a, 8; 29:44a, 45–46)

Yahweh has chosen the people of Israel from the beginning of the world, and has brought them out of dispersion and oppression so that he may take up his dwelling in their midst, and so that Israel's God-forsakenness may be ended for all time. The presence of God takes form in the cultic place which Israel is charged to establish.

We do not know where the Priestly source ended. It may possibly conclude with this fourth covenant promise, as if with a colon. But the completion of the sanctuary, which is described in Exodus 40, may also have belonged to it, even if only in a few confirmatory statements (verses 16, 34). Other possible conclusions, still under discussion, are the first sacrifice, in Leviticus 9, the great Day of Atonement, Leviticus 16, and the death of Moses, Deuteronomy 34.

The question about the end of the Priestly source goes together with the question about the importance that was attached to the promise of the land. In the promises to the patriarchs in the Priestly source, the land is emphasized to a striking degree. The topographical scheme is also at the service of this motif. Here the two themes of land and cult are complementary; for the significance of the promise of the land is that in its midst Yahweh will allow his Glory to have its dwelling. Because this is the place where Yahweh is encountered, it is the place where God's people have their given dwelling place.

Whether this was already part of the original stock of the Priestly source, or whether it belongs to the later additions, may remain an open question, especially since the complete conquest of the land and the "secure dwelling in the land" has at all times remained for the Jewish community an unattainable goal, for both external and internal reasons. The bitter polemic in the story about the spies in Numbers 13–14 throws light on the internal reasons. The spies bring back a malicious rumor about the country: "The land is a land that devours its inhabitants"; it offers no foundation for an existence. At that the Israelites grumble, and want to return to "the fleshpots of Egypt," in their secure diaspora existence. But Yahweh carries off the slanderous spies by means of a plague.

The *conquest of the land* itself is described in the books of Numbers and Joshua. The closeness of the account to the Priestly source, or to the books of Genesis to Numbers in their later compiled shape, is in many places obvious. But the account is not a factual historical record.

It is an attempt to compensate for the shortcomings of the present by way of an ideal early history. The war-like conquest as it is told here, together with the expulsion or "banishment" (in fact, the extermination) of the original non-Jewish inhabitants, never took place. It is nothing more than the claim of a religious minority to unrestricted possession of the land. It dates from a period when the believing Jewish community was compelled to share the land of Palestine with others. The list of the lands still unconquered (Judges 1:18–36) shows in unvarnished terms how little, even in the Persian-Hellenistic period, reality matched the claim.

𒀭

FIXING THE TORAH

The Pentateuch Redaction

The hypothesis that the Pentateuch—or, to be more precise, the narrative of the first four books of Moses, Genesis through Numbers—goes back to two originally independent written sources, the Yahwist's history (J) and the Priestly source (P), leads to a further assumption: that a redaction, or editorial revision, has woven these two works into the unity we have before us today.

The *aim* of this redaction was to get over the parallelism of the two accounts of salvation history. Yahweh's history with his people was a single history, so the written transmission of that history must have been a single one, too. Between the two narrative works there could be no difference as far as their validity as revelation is concerned. Their agreement in content was also certain. This agreement had to find visible expression in a literary unity.

Neither of the two documents had any a priori precedence. Their status demanded that both should be preserved as far as possible within the new whole. The former parallelism was overcome merely superficially in what, looked at closely, was a nonliterary way. The numerous roughnesses and contractions which resulted have made source-analysis (especially of the book of Genesis) one of the most obvious tasks for modern Old Testament criticism ever since the eighteenth century. The sources as individual literary entities were certainly lost in the process, but not their respective outlines of history. It is true that neither of the two sources can be reconstructed intact, but the theologically key texts, the chronological and genealogical scaffolding, as well as the characteristic narrative material, were as a whole probably preserved.

The unusual and laborious task of uniting two extensive authoritative texts into a third whole could only in fact be implemented if the *procedure* was as simple as possible: the sources that ran parallel to each other were placed one after the other, section by section. This is what was done with the Creation account: Genesis 1:1–2:4a (P) // Genesis 2:5–3:25 (J); with the genealogy between Creation and the Flood, Genesis 4 (J) // Genesis 5 (P); with the promise to Isaac, Genesis 17 (P) // Genesis 18:1–16 (J), with the announcement of the Exodus from Egypt, Exodus 3 (J) // Exodus 6 (P); and in many other cases.

Occasionally we can understand the reasoning of the redaction. It was obvious that the Creation account which opens, "In the beginning God created the heavens and the earth" (Gen. 1:1), would be put at the beginning. The other account was given simultaneity by way of the linking-phrase, "In the day when Yahweh God made the earth and the heavens" (Gen. 2:4b). At the same time that the event of the first account took place—the creation of earth and heaven—the second must also have taken its course. The two reports count as one and the same; it is just the viewpoint that has shifted. The first account establishes *that* man was created in the image of God (Gen. 1:27). The second is interpreted as the description of *the way* in which this happened: "Thus man became a living being" is the additional redactional comment (Gen. 2:7b), which lifts the term "living being" (Heb.: *næpæš ḥayyāh*) from the first account and carries it into the second.

The redaction deviated from this blocklike procedure only for compelling reasons. An exception of this kind is the story of the Flood (Gen. 6–9). There the reason is obvious: mankind could not have perished twice in succession. Consequently the two versions had to be dovetailed into a single account. From the eighteenth century onwards, the two were separated with considerable exegetical acumen and with ever increasing refinement. Two almost intact and highly contrasting accounts emerged. In one, the Flood is caused by an uninterrupted rain lasting forty days and forty nights. In the other, the primordial ocean surrounding the earth from above and below breaks in for 150 days, and the catastrophe lasts a year to the day. The sources are again dovetailed in a similar way in the story about the crossing of the sea and the destruction of the Egyptians (Exod. 14). This, too, could only be told once. But as a rule the parallel accounts are accepted.

In the primeval narrative, Genesis 1–11, the sources were blended on the foundation of the Priestly source, the text of the Yahwist's history being fitted into its closely structured framework. With the beginning of the story about the patriarchs in Genesis 12 this changes. From now on, until the beginning of the book of Exodus, the Yahwist's history provides the basis, because of its far more extensive material, the threads of the Priestly source being subsequently woven into its tapestry. In this way the literary structure of the Priestly source was for the most part lost. It is a question whether, in the story about the patriarchs, the Priestly source was ever an independent work, or whether it was not a supplementary commentary. But there are a number of cases where the fragments can be grafted together into a continuous thread.

It would probably be mistaken to ascribe to the redaction any more profound intention than a mere amalgamation of the sources. Respect for the revelatory character of the documents would not have permitted anything more. Nevertheless the *theological stature* of the existing text in its combined form should not be overlooked. It was not without justification that Franz Rosenzweig and Martin Buber expanded the siglum "R" (= redactor), which is generally used in exegesis, to *rabbenû* (Heb.: "our master"). This "mastery" can once again be seen from the example of the Creation accounts. It is only through the two taken together that the truth about the world and human beings unfolds: the optimistic rule over the world, *and* life on the thorny ground. Man is described as God's representative and steward, *and* as the one who broke the peace with God through his disobedience. "Have dominion over the earth" (Gen. 1:28); "You are dust, and to dust you shall return." (Gen. 3:19)

The text which came into being through the amalgamation of the Yahwist's history and the Priestly source was still far from being identical with the books of Genesis through Deuteronomy as we have them today. The portion of the text that was added afterwards is probably greater than the two former sources put together. The legal material is in many cases more recent, although it is sometimes impossible to decide whether the additions had already been part of the independent Priestly source. The growth is of such diversity that it cannot be grasped simply by assuming a planned "Pentateuch redaction."

The most extensive text to be added later was Deuteronomy. The accepted view used to be that Deuteronomy was already joined to the (expanded) Yahwist's history before the Priestly source was added, but this hypothesis is no longer held in more recent exegesis. A later step, even though it was certainly not the final one, was to divide the whole body of the text as it had developed into five books. A sharp caesura was inserted after the note about the death of Moses. The fivefold book was attributed to Moses as the mediator of revelation, and, as "the book of the Torah," a special, outstanding religious quality was ascribed to it, over against the rest of the Old Testament. We can deduce from the textual history that the Torah arrived at this special status around about the beginning of the Hellenistic era.

❄

THE MODIFICATION
OF KINGSHIP THEOLOGY

Second Isaiah

About half way through the book of Isaiah there is a caesura which is so marked that with Isaiah 40 what is really a new prophetic book begins. We are reminded of the amalgamation of independent prophetic books into a larger literary unit in the case of the book of the Twelve Prophets—except that in the book of Isaiah a separate title is missing. The caesura before Isaiah 40 is not the only one of its kind. There is another at the end of Isaiah 55, where utterances about the efficacy of God's word go together with Isaiah 40:1–8 to form a kind of framework. It has become usual to view Second Isaiah, or "Deutero-Isaiah" (Isa. 40–55), as an independent literary entity, with Third Isaiah, or "Trito-Isaiah" (Isa. 56–65) forming another. But the break between Isaiah 55 and 56 is less extreme, especially since Isaiah 55–66 does not constitute another independent literary unit. Recently, traces resembling Isaiah 40–66 have also been increasingly detected in Isaiah 1–39. These show that the book of Isaiah was in the end understood as a unity, not just as a collection.

Isaiah 40–55 is characterized by a unified style of its own. Because of that people liked to see "Second Isaiah" as a particular person, comparable with the eighth- and seventh-century prophets. The famous opening verses—"'Comfort, comfort my people,' says your God." "A voice says, 'Cry!' And I said, 'What shall I cry?'" (Isa. 40:1, 6)—were even seen as God's call to this anonymous prophet. But in this book the question about the person of the prophet is even less appropriate than it is elsewhere. Second Isaiah's individual character is due above all to the genres used. It is not an individual signature.

For a long time the *historical place* of the book seemed certain. In two passages, Isaiah 44:28 and 45:1, the Persian king Cyrus is mentioned by name, and is called Yahweh's instrument. It is in this light that other statements in the book are discussed as well: Yahweh will rouse a man who will come unopposed from the East (or North), and will subjugate peoples and kings. He will establish a rule of justice, and will rebuild the city of Jerusalem (Isa. 41:2, 25; 45:13; 46:11; 48:15). This seems to fit Cyrus's victorious campaign, which began in 550 BCE with the conquest of the Medes and reached its goal in 539 BCE with the conquest of Babylon.

It has meanwhile emerged, however, that the *sayings about Cyrus* were not originally part of Second Isaiah. We can see from 44:28 why they have been inserted. Yahweh commissions Cyrus to rebuild the Temple: "He is my shepherd, and he shall fulfil all my purposes, saying of Jerusalem, 'She shall be built!'

and of the temple, 'Your foundations shall be laid!'"
Behind this statement is a problem: the problem that
the postexilic Temple was no longer built as sanctuary
of the Jewish kings but was commissioned by the Persian overlord. The theological way out was to say that
Cyrus also acted on Yahweh's instructions. He is declared to be Yahweh's anointed one, as if he were an
offspring of the Davidic dynasty (Isa. 45:1).

However, the difficulty was not prompted by actual
history. It derives from the description found in the
book of Ezra, which dates only from the advanced
Persian period (see page 137). According to this, in his
victory over Babylon the founder of the Persian empire had no more important goal in view than the
restoration of the Jewish community in Jerusalem.
Without delay, he issues an edict ordering the return
of the exiled Judeans (the whole Jewish community is
in exile, according to this version) so that they may rebuild the temple (2 Chron. 36 // Ezra 1). But in fact
under Cyrus Persian domination had not yet reached
as far as Palestine. The Temple was built only under
Darius, between 520 and 515 BCE, and the exilic
Judeans did not play a prominent part in its rebuilding. Because the account in the book of Ezra does not
record historical events as they actually took place, it
has to explain the delay in building the Temple in a
convoluted way.

The Cyrus references in Isaiah 44:28 and 45:1, then,
rest on a picture of history deriving from the advanced Persian period which has theological reasons
behind it, not historical ones; to leave out the Cyrus

references lays bare the meaning of the earlier text. It means that the date of Second Isaiah can no longer be deduced from external criteria. The closeness to the language and thought of the Psalms strongly suggests that the book originated in the vicinity of the Jerusalem Temple. It is not the people in exile who are addressed here; it is the postexilic community. The dispersion, where it is mentioned, is worldwide.

The core of the book is to be found in the Isaiah section 40–48, beginning with 40:12. Two genres are prominent: the disputation speech and the salvation oracle. The *disputation speech* could also be called a pleading, like an address in court. Here it is the speech of the defense—its "apologia," theologically speaking, or vindication. The people addressed are the peoples of the world as well as the other gods, but above all the doubts of the readers and listeners themselves. An appeal is made to their judgment and conviction:

> Who has measured the waters in the hollow of his
>   hand,
> and marked off the heavens with a span, . . .
> and weighed the mountains in scales
> and the hills in a balance? . . .
>> Behold, the nations are like a drop from a
>>   bucket,
>> and are accounted as the dust on the scales. . . .
> Have you not known? Have you not heard?
> Has it not been told you from the beginning? . . .
>> Why do you say, O Jacob,
>> and speak, O Israel,
>> "My way is hid from Yahweh,

and my right is disregarded by my God?"
Have you not known? Have you not heard?
Yahweh is an everlasting God,
the Creator of the ends of the earth. . . .
He gives power to the faint,
and to him who has no might he increases
strength. . . .
I am Yahweh, the first, and with the last: I am He.
(Isa. 40:12*, 15a, 21a, 27–28a*, 29; 41:4b)

The statements are put in the form of questions: "Have you not known?" An appeal is made to already existing knowledge ("told you from the beginning"), knowledge in which experience of nature and history coincides with the traditional creed. The appeal to this knowledge is supposed to overcome the doubt; for despair and profound distress say that God takes no note of his people's fate.

The doubt seems to apply to Yahweh's ability to act, however, rather than to his will. Hence the appeal, "Have you not known? Have you not heard?" and the reminder that Yahweh has created the ends of the earth. The answer towards which everything tends is the triumphant self-revelation, "I, Yahweh, am the first, and with the last I am He." The statement can count as a motto for the whole book of Second Isaiah (cf. 44:6 and 48:12). The person of the Supreme God, to whom the creation of heaven and earth is attributed, reveals himself as "Yahweh": "I am Yahweh and there is no other" (Isa. 45:18). This religious equation can easily be understood against the background of world-wide Persian domination.

Together with Yahweh's role, the role of his people changes, too. God's emphatic "I" addresses a "You":

> But you, Israel, my servant,
> Jacob, whom I have chosen: . . .
> Fear not, for I am with you;
> be not dismayed, for I am your God. . . .
> Behold, all who are incensed against you
> shall be put to shame and confounded;
> those who strive against you
> shall be as nothing and shall perish. . . .
> For I, Yahweh your God,
> hold your right hand;
> it is I who say to you, "Fear not,
> I will help you." (Isa. 41:8–13*; cf. Isa. 43:1–7)

The genre pattern in which this assurance is framed is the *salvation oracle,* in the cult proclaimed to the individual petitioner and especially to the king (see page 48). But here it is the people as a whole who are addressed. The longing for the restoration of the Davidic kingdom is met by the curious solution that the function of Yahweh's *royal servant* is transferred from the individual king to God's people. This mental leap was made possible in that Israel is now addressed as an individual, the people of God being identified with its forefather, Jacob.

Just as the king was set over the people by Yahweh, it is now Israel who becomes the vassal of the universal Supreme God, acting on his behalf towards the world of the nations:

> Behold my servant, whom I uphold,
> my chosen, in whom my soul delights. . . .

> He will bring forth justice to the nations, . . .
> and the coastlands wait for his law. (Isa. 42:1–4*)

Just as the king rules and pacifies the country by exercising justice and giving instructions, thus fulfilling the commission given him by the deity, in the same way Israel will now carry Yahweh's law to the ends of the earth and, commissioned by him, will rule and pacify the whole world of the nations. This tremendous religious self-presumption mirrors the factual unimportance of a Temple community, divested of all political power, on the margin of the worldwide Persian Empire.

The central statement in Second Isaiah has later been varied in a number of ways. Particular attention has naturally been paid to the role of the Servant. The passage just cited is considered in exegesis to be the first of the four *Servant of God songs* (Isa. 42:1–4; 49:1–6; 50:4–9; 52:13–53:12), which many scholars view as a separate literary entity within the book of Second Isaiah. But in fact the four passages do not share the same literary origin. Having been, at the beginning, part of Second Isaiah's apologia, in the course of time the motif has developed backwards, so to speak, the collective being given an individual meaning: the royal servant became the righteous sufferer, and his mission to the world of the nations the vicarious suffering for the many.

The *Zion* theme also became part of the book of Second Isaiah only at a later date. Essentially speaking, it is confined to the framework Isaiah 40:9–11 and Isaiah 49–55. Now the main emphasis lies on the direct rule of God. Jerusalem has been deserted by its

God, and waits in fearful longing for his return, as a city waits for its king, who has gone to war for an incalculable time. The messengers of joy on the mountains, and the watchers on the battlements, announce his imminent return: "Behold, your God is coming to his ancestral kingdom as a victor laden with the spoils of war, and as good shepherd and king" (Isa. 40:9–11; 52:7–9). From this time on, longing for the kingdom of God was of determining importance for faith.

CHAPTER 12

PROPHETIC ESCHATOLOGY

The Book of Isaiah

Traditionally the book of Isaiah has counted as the quintessential prophetic book. No other prophetic writing enjoyed a comparable status either in early Christianity or in Qumran. It therefore shows in an exemplary way how the prophetic books developed into their present form, and how they arrived at their present significance.

Only a small part of the first part of the book ("Proto-Isaiah," chapters 1–39) goes back to the prophet Isaiah himself. The account of his call, which very probably initiated the earliest collection, can today be found only in chapter 6. How much this call-scene determined the picture which came to be held about Isaiah's prophecy can be seen from the heading which calls the whole book "the vision of Isaiah" (Isa. 1:1). It follows from this that the opening chapters came to precede the call at a later point—either because they were written later, or because they have been shifted from somewhere else in the book. The call was probably followed initially by the symbolic action in Isaiah 8 (see page 54). The earliest book will doubtless have contained other prophetic sayings, but it is not easy to say which sayings they were. In accordance with the role of cult prophet, the original message predicts disaster for Judah's enemies. These enemies included the Northern Kingdom of Israel. But when, in the seventh century BCE, Judah set about appropriating the traditions and self-understanding of the North, thus claiming to be itself "Israel," and when it then fell to the Neo-Babylonians in the sixth century BCE, the message was all at once read as if Isaiah had prophesied in Yahweh's name the downfall of his own people. This step determined the tradition from then on.

The origin continued to affect the late expansions inasmuch as the whole book centers on the theme of Zion, the cultic site where the prophet was active. The book of Isaiah has been called the book about the threat to Zion and her preservation. This concentration was probably influenced both by the recollection that in 701 BCE Jerusalem had been unexpectedly saved from the Assyrian conquest, and by the remembrance of the annihilation of the Temple and the Davidic dynasty in 586 BCE. The book looks ever more resolutely beyond the plight and impending danger of the postexilic present into the future. The expectations are dominated by the idea of a fundamental turn of events which will decisively change for the better the living conditions of the present, indeed to some degree will put an end to the course of history itself.

The movement of the whole book leads from disaster for Israel (Isa. 1:12), by way of disaster for the nations (Isa. 13–23), to Israel's final salvation. This movement determines the book as a totality, but characterizes smaller units as well, such as the sequence

Isaiah 9–12: Yahweh will punish the faithless Northern Kingdom, or those who have succeeded to it (Isa. 9:7–10:4); Assyria (or Syria, the empire of the Seleucids which succeeded to it in Hellenistic times) will be defeated by its enemies (Isa. 10:5–19); the holy remnant which dwells on Zion will experience the destruction of Assyria as their ancestors once experienced the destruction of the Egyptians in the sea (Isa. 10:20–34). Then the Davidic dynasty will rise up again: a shoot from the stump of Jesse which had been hewn down (Isa. 11:1–5, 9). A rule of righteousness and justice will begin. In the end the future takes on completely utopian features:

> The wolf shall dwell with the lamb,
> and the leopard shall lie down with the kid,
> and the calf and the lion and the fatling together,
> and a little child shall lead them.
> The cow and the bear shall feed;
> their young shall lie down together;
> and the lion shall eat straw like the ox.
> The sucking child shall play over the hole of the
> asp,
> and the weaned child shall put his hand on the
> adder's den. (Isa. 11:6–8)

The people of God will stream in from the whole earth and gather round Zion. The enmity between the former Northern Kingdom and the South will also be ended (Isa. 11:10–16). The composition flows into the hymn of thanksgiving of the redeemed, who proclaim Yahweh's marvelous acts to the nations of the world (Isa. 12:1–6).

We find a similar sequence, which is virtually a drama of world history, in Isaiah 28ff., at the end of which the redeemed return home to Zion, and Zion itself becomes paradise (Isa. 35). This anticipates Isaiah 40–66, so that the close of today's whole book, with its prophecy of salvation, also appears as a component part of the great historical drama.

The expectations of the future vary widely. Individually they are mutually contradictory: parallel to the deliverance of God's people stands the deliverance only of the remnant which has remained true to Yahweh, and the terrible punishment of the leaders of the people, especially the Temple priesthood. Parallel to the return of the Davidic kings stands the direct rule of God, as universal kingdom of peace. Parallel to the annihilation of the nations stands their repentance and turn to Yahweh:

> It shall come to pass in the latter days
> that the mountain of the house of Yahweh
> shall be established as the highest of the
>   mountains,
> and shall be raised above the hills;
> and all the nations shall flow to it,
> and many peoples shall come. . . .
> They shall beat their swords into ploughshares,
> and their spears into pruning hooks;
> nation shall not lift up sword against nation,
> neither shall they learn war any more. . . .
> And Yahweh will reign over them . . .
> from this time forth and for evermore. (Isa. 2:2–5*,
>   from Micah 4:1–7*)

Finally, we find the revival of the age-old ideas that the cosmos is going to sink back into the chaos from which it was wrested when the world began (cf. Gen. 1–3; 6–9). No one will escape:

> He who flees at the sound of the terror
> shall fall into the pit;
> and he who climbs out of the pit
> shall be caught in the snare.
> For the windows of heaven are opened,
> and the foundations of the earth tremble.
> The earth is utterly broken,
> the earth is rent asunder,
> the earth is violently shaken. (Isa. 24:18–19)

This theme is developed in Isaiah 24–27, a composition which is obviously late, and which scholars have therefore detached from the rest of the book, giving it the name of the "Isaiah apocalypse." This is the beginning of the path which led to the fully developed apocalyptic of the second century BCE (see page 165).

In the midst of the chaos that breaks in, Zion, the mountain of God, remains unscathed and becomes the refuge of the righteous. Since it is obedience to Yahweh that alone decides over the deliverance, the borderline between Israel and the other nations loses its importance. All are invited to the banquet on the mountain of God in the last days (cf. Exod. 24:9–11):

> On this mountain Yahweh Sabaoth will make
>   for all peoples
> a feast of fat things,
> a feast of well-aged wine,

of fat things full of marrow,
of well-aged wine well refined.
And he will destroy on this mountain
the covering that is cast over all peoples,
the veil that is spread over all nations.
He will swallow up death for ever,
and the Lord Yahweh will wipe away tears
    from all faces,
and the reproach of his people he will take
    away from all the earth;
for Yahweh has spoken. (Isa. 25:6–8)

A vision such as this holds out the ultimate prospect of an unconditioned community with God for all mankind, and its final redemption.

CHAPTER 13

✶❀✶

THE CONFLICT WITH THE
PROTO-SAMARITAN COMMUNITY

The Book of Hosea

The history of Israel and Judah has at all times been marked by an antithesis between north and south, and this is true of their religious history, too. Israel, as the single, unified people of God, has never been more than a political and religious ideal born in the late period. Even under David and Solomon, there was merely a personal union. It is true that in the ninth century BCE the Davidic kings were close allies of the Omrides, but more often the kingdoms stood in open conflict to one another. The Northern Kingdom was always predominant. That this superiority did not continuously make itself felt was due only to the fact that the North was more exposed to Assyrian pressure, and succumbed to it earlier. But after the South had also lost its sovereignty, the different weight of the two became evident once more. The books of Ezra and Nehemiah report that the building of the Second Temple, as well as of the city walls, was considerably impeded from the side of Samaria. The historical details may be uncertain, but the conflict was clearly a fact. At a date we do not know, this led to the Samaritan schism: the sanctuary on Mount Garizim near Shechem became the center for the Samaritan community, which refused to pay allegiance to the Temple in Jerusalem.

This must have led to vigorous polemic on Jerusalem's side, since on the basis of Deuteronomy it claimed sole religious representation. This polemic has probably been preserved in part. In the Old Testament it had its appropriate place in the writings whose message had always been directed against the Northern Kingdom: the books of the prophets Hosea and Amos. If we read the book of Hosea in particular from this aspect, much of what it says becomes astonishingly transparent. The polemic against the sanctuaries of Bethel and Gilgal in the book of Amos (Amos 3:14; 4:4–5; 5:5–6, 21–24) also probably had its roots here.

The book of Hosea falls into two parts, which are uneven in length. Hosea 1–3 deals with the prophet's marriage and his children. Hosea 4–14 is a great collection of oracles, which is again divided at the end of Hosea 11. The symbolic action in Hosea 1, an imitation of Isaiah 8:1–4 (see page 54), was probably occasioned, like its model, by the attack of Aram and Israel on Jerusalem in 734 or 733 BCE. At some later point the symbolic action has been placed in front of an already existing collection of prophetic sayings. This emerges from the redaction's comment in Hosea 1:2, which defines the action as "the beginning of Yahweh's speech to Hosea," which it was not originally. The earlier beginning can be found in Hosea 4:

The word of Yahweh that came to Hosea the son of Beeri. . . . Hear the word of Yahweh, O people of

Israel; for Yahweh has a controversy with the inhabitants of the land. . . . Swearing, lying, killing, stealing and committing adultery have broken all bounds in the land, and murder follows murder. (Hos. 1:1*; 4:1–2*)

The series of offenses (which later became the germ of the Decalogue; see page 88) has a possible continuation in Hosea 10:4:

They utter mere words; with empty oaths they make covenants; so judgment springs up like poisonous weeds in the furrows of the field.

We cannot be certain where this polemic originated; it is linked with Hosea only through the (later) heading. The prophet as a person is nowhere mentioned again.

The style is declaratory: accusations are made. The model is the speech before the court of law (Hos. 2:2; 4:1, 4; 12:2). Taken literally, it is Yahweh who has a "controversy" with the Northern Kingdom. Who was it, who claimed God for his own interests in this way? The supposition that Hosea was the exponent of "opposition groups" in the Northern Kingdom is not very probable. But perhaps the polemic can nevertheless be understood in the context of the eighth century BCE, as springing from the enmity that dominated relations between North and South just before the end of the Northern Kingdom. This would also fit in with such an assertion as, "In the dawn the king of Israel shall be utterly cut off" (Hos. 10:15b).

Understood in this sense, the polemic would have originated in Judah. At all events, after the fall of

Samaria, the book must have been further transmitted in the South. Its core can probably be found in chapters 4 (at the beginning), 7, and 9–10. It was only in the post-exilic period that it grew to its present size through insertions and appendices.

A first major expansion can be found in some ominous symbolic oracles about Ephraim:

> Ephraim's glory shall fly away like a bird. . . .
> Ephraim, I have seen it like a palm, planted on a
>   green meadow. . . .
> Ephraim is stricken. Their root is dried up,
> they shall bear no fruit. (Hos. 9:11–16*)

Utterances such as these suggest an origin in the fifth/fourth century rather than in the eighth/seventh. They can easily be understood as dating from the time when Judah claimed to be Israel, and therefore denied to the North its hereditary name, which was replaced by the geographical term "Ephraim."

Later, particular attention is directed to the cult and its institutions. Hosea 4:4–10 focuses the accusation in 4:1–3* on "the priest," disputing his legitimacy. The priests have become a net and a snare for the common people (Hos. 5:1). We can sense the fury over the disagreeable rivals who permitted themselves to interpret Deuteronomy in their own way. They hinder the pilgrimages to the South, and seize for themselves cultic contributions claimed by the Temple in Jerusalem (Hos. 4:8). It is a question whether "Gilead" and "Gilgal," as well as "Beth-aven" (=Bethel), against whom the polemic is directed (Hos. 4:15; 5:8; 6:8; 9:15; 10:5, 8, 15; 12:12), are code names. In these places Yahweh will not let himself be found. The sacrifices are null and void, indeed acts of sacrilege. Finally the backsliding from the cult in Jerusalem is equated with backsliding from Yahweh. It is whoredom.

The North is reproached for its politics, too. The strict separation from the Gentiles is not observed. Diplomatic feelers are stretched out to Ptolemaic Egypt and Seleucid Syria:

> Ephraim mixes himself with the peoples. . . .
> Aliens devour his strength, and he knows it not. . . .
> They call to Egypt, they go to Assyria. (Hos. 7:8–11*)

Like the nefarious inhabitants of Gibeah (cf. Judg. 19–20), Ephraim has cut itself off from the association of God's people through its sins (Hos. 9:9; 10:9). Yahweh will cast them off as he cast off Saul (Hos. 9:17; cf. 1 Sam. 15), so that they will be fugitives among the nations, like Cain (cf. Gen. 4). For them, salvation history will be annihilated from the beginning.

CHAPTER 14

꙰

JUDAISM ON THE THRESHOLD OF THE HELLENISTIC AGE

The Chronicler's History

As well as the great historical work which comprises the books from Genesis through Kings, the Old Testament contains yet another account of the history of God's people: the so-called Chronicler's History. The customary name goes back to Jerome. The Hebrew term *dibrê hayyāmîm* means literally "(Book of) Occurrences." The work describes yet again the course of history from the beginning of mankind until the Babylonian exile. It ends with the edict of the Persian king Cyrus, which orders the rebuilding of the Temple. The books of Ezra and Nehemiah, linked through the repetition of the Cyrus edict, include the history of the postexilic community in the fifth century BCE.

In this new history, the interpretation of the given tradition is no longer inserted into the already existing text, but has given rise to a separate, parallel work. The attitude to earlier tradition has changed: now a distinction is made between the sacred text and its interpretation. Although it is still included in the Old Testament, the Chronicler's History understands itself as being deutero-canonical. We might call it an early "midrash." It is not without reason that in many Hebrew manuscripts it comes right at the end. In others it forms the "historical" introduction to the Psalms.

The Chronicler understands the history of God's people as the history of the Davidic monarchy. The period of time from Adam to Saul is bridged by genealogies, which have been elicited from the books of Genesis and Numbers. It is only with the death of Saul that the narrative begins. The basis is provided by the books of Samuel and Kings. As far as we can see, the numerous and varied source-references refer only to the familiar canonical books. It has often been assumed that for the descriptions which go beyond what is told in Samuel and Kings, the Chronicler has other sources at his disposal. If this were so, it would considerably augment our knowledge about the preexilic period. But it is improbable. It would be rash to rely on a document deriving from the Hellenistic age for a reconstruction of the history of the monarchical period.

The account identifies the monarchy in Israel and Judah with the Davidic dynasty. But it sees the main task of the kings as care of the Temple. The founder of the dynasty is presented as the devout founder of the Temple cult. All the somber features, such as David's struggle with Saul, the rivalry about the succession, and even his adultery, are excluded. Other than in the books of Kings, David even makes the building of the Temple his own concern to such an extent that for Solomon only the very last act of its implementation is left.

After the separation of the Northern and Southern kingdoms, the account confines itself exclusively to the kings of Judah. The Northern Kingdom might not have existed at all. New narrative material compensates for the radical cuts. Whereas the books of Kings supply no more than a mere chronological scaffolding for the kings of Judah, the Chronicler offers detailed narratives. But the subjects of these expansions alone show that they are constructions: building activities, and wars following the ideal pattern of the Holy War.

With expansions of this kind the Chronicler also pursues the goal of showing the effectiveness of Yahweh's justice. For this purpose the history follows the judgments about the piety of the monarchs which it found in the books of Kings. The doctrine says that devout kings are successful, and kings who sin against the Torah are unsuccessful. If kings are successful, they must have been devout; if they fail, it was because they sinned against the Torah. This viewpoint now comes to prevail: it is the picture of God which creates the picture of history. Thus devout kings who are unsuccessful are retrospectively accused of apostasy, like Jehoash, who fell victim to a plot (2 Kings 12 // 2 Chron. 24). Manasseh, however, reigned for fifty-five years in spite of his godlessness (1 Kings 21), so he must in the meantime have repented (2 Chron. 33).

The center of the world is the Temple in Jerusalem. This is not surprising in the postexilic period. What is new is the awakened interest in the monarchy. However unpolitical the account may be, the Judah settled round the Temple receives a religious and political identity. Hopes like this for political independence could well have sprung up when world politics were in a phase of upheaval, as they were after Alexander's death, for example. The striking limitation to Judah can be intended as a dissociation from the Samaritan community.

An interpretation of the original outline is made more difficult because, like all the biblical writings, the Chronicler's History has acquired additions. The genealogies and the details about the establishment of the cult cried out for later amplification. The conviction about God's just vengeance has led, step by step, to the addition of further details.

The link with the books of *Ezra* and *Nehemiah* was probably also made at a later date. The two books originally formed a coherent work. The basis of the first part of Ezra-Nehemiah is an Aramaic narrative which aims to trace back the rebuilding of the Temple (which actually took place under Darius I) to Cyrus's decree (Ezra 5:1–6:15). The second part rests on Nehemiah's memorandum, which is written in an autobiographical style (Neh. 1–7*; 12–13*). Nehemiah was the cupbearer of Artaxerxes I (465/64–425 BCE). In the twentieth year of the king's reign (= 445/44 BCE) Nehemiah persuaded Artaxerxes to commission him to journey to Jerusalem, and there to order the rebuilding of the city walls. The report of a well-placed Persian official is a historical source of the first importance for the middle of the fifth century BCE. It has a parallel, dating from 519/18 BCE, in the inscription of the Egyptian physician Udjahorresne, who was in the employ of Cambyses and Darius I (AEL 3. 36–41).

In their present form, the books of Ezra and Nehemiah describe the establishment of the postexilic community. The earlier Cyrus edict is antedated in Ezra 1 (= 2 Chron. 36) by a later Hebrew version, which orders the return of the exiles as precondition for the building of the Temple. According to this account, postexilic Israel emerged only from the Babylonian exilic community. The Jews already living in Jerusalem are compelled to separate from their non-Jewish wives. After the building of the walls has been completed (as well as all the other necessary building), Ezra reads aloud the Torah to the people (Neh. 8). The scene is expanded by a prayer of repentance (Neh. 9) and a solemn commitment to obedience (Neh. 10).

CHAPTER 15

※※

SECTS AND GROUPS
WITHIN HELLENISTIC JUDAISM

From the second half of the Persian era there began to
be a social differentiation within the Jewish community in and around Jerusalem, which ultimately led to
the crystallization of distinct groups. Late postexilic Judaism was much less unified than it appears to be
in retrospect. The division which is historically dis-
cernible in the first century BCE, with the Pharisees, the
Sadducees and the Essenes, was heralded long before.
For this division there were practical reasons, among
other things. From the Persian era onwards, the outcome of economic development was the growth of a
poverty-stricken class in Judah. If we follow Nehemiah
5, a real social crisis resulted. Apparently the law about
debt remission in Leviticus 25 was occasioned by de-
velopments of this kind.

The poor took their neediness to be the proof of a
special closeness to God. They combined their poverty
with an intense piety. We find the literary traces of this
in the late strata of the prophetic books and their social criticism, occasionally even in the Torah, but
above all in the Writings. Important books belonging
to this third part of the Old Testament canon were in
the end edited no longer at the Temple school but by

these devout groups. It is not without reason that rabbinic Judaism as the transmitter of Old Testament tradition is heir to such a group, the Pharisees. The most important examples for that input are the Psalter and the book of Proverbs.

THE PSALTER

The collection as we have it contains exactly 150 psalms. The round number was arrived at by splitting up individual psalms and putting others together. In the Septuagint and, following that, in the Vulgate, this rearrangement differed slightly from the arrangement in the Hebrew Bible (which sometimes leads to confusion in liturgical practice). By the beginning of the first century BCE, the Psalter had probably arrived at its present extent, although the contours were still not fully defined: the Septuagint contains a further, unnumbered psalm, the Peshitta five additional ones. The prayer book of a living community of faith is never static. This is also shown by later compilations, such as the psalm scroll found in Cave 11 in Qumran.

Basically, the Psalter is a *collection of collections*. These earlier collections can be recognized from the psalm headings, information which can sometimes be read as filing notes. When the collections were put together in the larger Psalter, they had already to some extent become fixed. Psalms which appeared in several collections remained as doublets (e.g., Ps. 14 // Ps. 53).

The composition is also given a new, deeper meaning. For example, the royal psalms, 2 and 89, form a frame which sets an earlier form of the Psalter under the theme "messianic hope." The "Yahweh is King" psalms, 93–100, some of which are very old indeed, form an appendix to this, and contribute the theo-cratic viewpoint. Finally, there are signs of substantial revision. We find the clearest indication of this in Psalm 1, which opens the collection as we now have it like a motto:

> Blessed is the man
> who walks not in the counsel of the wicked,
> nor stands in the way of sinners,
> nor sits in the seat of scoffers;
> but his delight is in the law of Yahweh,
> and on his law he meditates day and night.
> He is like a tree planted by streams of water,
> that yields its fruit in its season,
> and its leaf does not wither.
> In all that he does, he prospers.
> The wicked are not so,
> but are like chaff which the wind drives away.
> Therefore the wicked will not stand in the
>   judgment,
> nor sinners in the congregation of the righteous;
> for Yahweh knows the way of the righteous,
> but the way of the wicked will perish.

This reader's guide sets the Psalter under the domi-nating theme of the contrast between the righteous and the wicked. The righteous will flourish. Every-thing they do prospers, for Yahweh knows their way. But the wicked are chaff. Their way will perish. We sense that in his picture of the righteous man the author is portraying what he sees himself to be: a man bent heart and soul on the study of the Torah. But he has doubts whether obedience will be rewarded: on the horizon is God's eschatological Judgment.

The theme recurs with variations in more than half of the psalms. It can in most cases be put down to literary revision. Additional notes of this kind are like traces of intensive use. Sometimes the genres thereby lose their original shape. The place of the Psalter changed from the worship of the congregation to the Bible-reading of the devout, and became the foundation for religious assurance and instruction.

There are other groups as well as the righteous. The humble (Heb.: *Anawim*) or the poor (Heb.: *Ebionim*) have adopted a considerable number of psalms for themselves. One example is the beginning of Psalm 86:

> Incline your ear, Yahweh, and answer me,
> *for I am humble and poor.*
> Preserve my life, for
> *I am godly. Save your servant,*
> you are my God.
> *who trusts in you.*
> Be gracious to me, Yahweh,
> for to you do I cry all the day.

The original psalm's invocation, petition, and expression of trust were later expanded by what the petitioner says about himself. This confuses the sequence of statements, which no Bible translation leaves uncorrected. The statement about himself, "for I am humble and poor," is found no less than seven times in the Psalter. In using it, the petitioner is not so much describing his own personal plight as identifying himself as member of a group which has a particular relationship to Yahweh. The attitude of humility proves itself in faithful obedience, in expectation of the eschatological Judgment.

Another group of this kind are the "faithful" (Heb.: *Hasidim, Hasideans),* whose important role in the Maccabean uprising in the second century BCE is known to us from 1 Macc. 2:42. In their case, humility is replaced by a militant faithfulness to Yahweh (cf. Ps. 149). In Psalm 30, which has later been entitled "A Song at the Dedication of the Temple" (which according to tradition means the Maccabean dedication of the Temple, *Chanukkah),* the Hasidim are added in verses 4-5:

> Sing praises to Yahweh, *O you his faithful,*
> and give thanks to his holy name.
> For his anger is but for a moment,
> and his favor is for a lifetime.
> Weeping may tarry for the night,
> but joy comes with the morning.

The addition is a rejoicing over the end of the devastation of the Temple. It was in these same groups that the book of Daniel originated.

THE BOOK OF PROVERBS

This, too, is a collection of collections (see page 33). The collection 10:1–22:16 probably formed the basic stock of the book, the others being added gradually.

The opening, Proverbs 1–9, in the light of which the book is intended to be read today, is a late addition.

The growth of the collection goes hand in hand with a historical development in ideas. An important step had to do with Yahweh's involvement. The traditional wisdom of experience got along without God—just like today's natural sciences and even education. This did not make it simply secular, but an occasion was needed for the religions dimension to be mentioned. This happens first when the possibility of an explanation comes up against its limits. For example, there is the difference between what one intends and what one does, which is a riddle even to the person concerned: "A man's mind plans his way, but Yahweh alone directs his steps" (Prov. 16:9). This is especially awkward in the case of public speaking: "The plans of the mind belong to man, but the answer of the tongue is from Yahweh" (Prov. 16:1). The difference between perceiving and understanding, which is difficult to comprehend, is traced back to Yahweh: "The hearing ear and the seeing eye, Yahweh has made them both" (Prov. 20:12). The same may be said of the existing difference in prosperity: "The rich and the poor meet together; Yahweh is the maker of them all" (Prov. 22:2). Even official decisions are incalculable: "The king's heart is a stream of water in the hand of Yahweh; he turns it wherever he will" (Prov. 21:1).

We find a later form of specifically theological wisdom in Proverbs 1–9. Whether this collection ever existed independently, or whether it came into being as the opening for the book of Proverbs, is uncertain. It rests on ten didactic speeches, which are built up on a particular pattern. The pupil is addressed as "my son." What is passed on here is not so much specific rules for living as an attitude of mind: the turn to wisdom as such, which means the same thing as the turn to Yahweh. Considerable space is devoted to the insistent warning against adultery, and the admonition to remain faithful to the woman wedded in one's youth (Prov. 5:1–14; 6:20–35; 7:1–23). Faithfulness to one's wife, the constant adherence to wisdom, and faithfulness to Yahweh go hand in hand. In Proverbs 1:20–33 and 8:12–36 Wisdom is personified as a woman, and she herself speaks. The order of the world is evidence that she was already present when the world was created, and that God let himself be guided by her (8:22–31).

The closeness of wisdom to piety which begins here increased considerably in the late period. There are signs that the book of Proverbs was eagerly read by the devout. This was no accident; for the attention of the devout was fastened on the connection between act and destiny, as it was in ancient wisdom. The standard was the Torah; the theological principle was the righteousness of God. In a certain sense these proverbs can be read as prophetic promises. The vanishing point towards which everything tends is the divine Judgment.

As in the Psalter, a kind of schematic "typing" emerges: the righteous man who lives according to God's will is contrasted with the wicked man, who does not do so. In the light of this viewpoint the proverbs were copiously expanded. The righteous man expects that his way of life, which conforms to the will of God, will be rewarded by success in life.

Instead, his fate is no different from that of everyone else; indeed it is often worse, and he has to look on as those who contravene God's will have an easier and happier life. The outlet was ultimately the idea of a compensatory justice after death. This was the motivation for a hope for the world beyond, a hope which increasingly determined Jewish faith from the Hellenistic period onwards.

CHAPTER 16

🙢🙠

DIDACTIC STORIES

In the late postexilic period the didactic story was a genre that came to be fairly widespread. Theological problems—but the proper behavior towards God, too—were worked out on the basis of exemplary situations, which were usually exaggerated. Paradigms of this kind are frequent in the late additions to the book of Genesis (e.g., "Abraham with Abimelech," Gen. 20; "the sacrifice of Isaac," Gen. 22; "Dinah," Gen. 34; "Judah and Tamar," Gen. 38). They are favorites in the deutero-canonical literature, too. Three of them have become separate books in the Hebrew canon.

JONAH

This is the only book in the book of the Twelve Prophets which is a story *about* a prophet, not a collection of prophetic sayings. The nucleus of the story was as follows:

> Now the word of Yahweh came to Jonah the son of Amittai, saying, "Arise, go to Nineveh, that great city, and cry against it; for their wickedness has come up before me." . . . So Jonah arose and went to Nineveh, according to the word of Yahweh. . . . And

> he cried, "Yet forty days, and Nineveh shall be over-
> thrown!" Then the people of Nineveh believed God;
> they proclaimed a fast, and put on sackcloth from
> the greatest of them to the least of them. . . . When
> God saw what they did, how they turned from their
> evil way, God repented of the evil which he had
> said he would do to them; and he did not do it.
> (Jonah 1:1–2; 3:3a, 4b–5, 10)

This is an invented example, a test case. It illustrates
the reward of contrition: repentance will turn away
God's judgment. Underlying the story is a theology of
history, in which the call to repentance, as it is found in
the later shape of the prophetic books, coalesces with
the doctrine about the justice of everything God does:

> If at any time I declare concerning a nation or a
> kingdom, that I will pluck up and break down and
> destroy it, and if that nation . . . turns from its evil, I
> will repent of the evil that I intended to do to it.
> And if at any time I declare concerning a nation or
> a kingdom that I will build and plant it, and if it
> does evil in my sight, not listening to my voice,
> then I will repent of the good which I had intended
> to do to it. (Jer. 18:7–10)

The general applicability of a doctrinal tenet is proved
by the extreme case. That is why the example chosen is
the capital city of Assyria, the great power to which the
Northern Kingdom of Israel has fallen victim. The
threat is passed on by the last prophet to be named
in the book of 2 Kings before the downfall of the Northern Kingdom: Jonah, son of Amittai, who according to

2 Kings 14:25 preached under King Jeroboam II. The scene follows a pattern which is familiar from the Elijah stories in 1 Kings 17 and from the symbolic actions in Jeremiah 13 and Jeremiah 18. The call for repentance is successful, and the rule is applied: Nineveh is spared.

The unimpeachable theological theory was not endorsed by the natural reaction, however. In a further step, the objection is put into Jonah's mouth:

> But this displeased Jonah exceedingly, and he was angry. And he prayed to Yahweh and said, "I pray you, Yahweh, is not this what I said when I was yet in my country? . . . For I knew that you are a gracious God and merciful, slow to anger, and abounding in steadfast love, and that you repent of evil. Therefore now, Yahweh, take my life from me, I beseech you, for it is better for me to die than to live." And Yahweh said: "Do you do well to be angry?" (Jon. 4:1, 2*, 3–4)

Of course a flaw has crept into the reasoning: the point of the original story is God's justice, but Jonah complains about Yahweh's grace—as if God were tempering justice with mercy. In response, Jonah is asked a question, which is of course meant for the reader. Yahweh repeats it again later in the story when, taking the example of a castor oil plant, he tries to convince Jonah to accept the divine readiness to forgive.

Later, Jonah's resistance has been placed at the very beginning of the story. When he hears Yahweh's charge, he flees in the opposite direction: instead of going to Nineveh, he tries to escape by sea. But a storm gets up. The sailors throw the man who is responsible for it into the sea. A great fish rescues Jonah and spits him out on land. Now Yahweh again sends him to Nineveh. The theme has numerous parallels in the literature of antiquity, for example in the saga of Perseus and Andromeda. The great fish—the text leaves its species open—has made the book of Jonah one of the most popular parts of the Old Testament.

JOB

In its dramatic power and theological profundity the book is unparalleled, and not in the Bible alone. It grew out of the following story:

> There was a man in the land of Uz, whose name was Job; and that man was blameless and upright, one who feared God, and turned away from evil. . . . He had seven thousand sheep, three thousand camels, five hundred yoke of oxen, and five hundred she-asses, and very many servants; so that this man was the greatest of all the people of the east. . . . Now there was a day . . . when there came a messenger to Job, and said, "The oxen were ploughing and the asses feeding beside them; and the Sabeans fell upon them and took them, and slew the servants with the edge of the sword; and I alone have escaped to tell you." While he was yet speaking, there came another, and said, "The fire of God fell from heaven and burned up the sheep and the servants, and consumed them; and I alone have escaped to tell you." While he was yet speaking, there came

another, and said, "The Chaldeans formed three
companies, and made a raid upon the camels and
took them, and slew the servants with the edge
of the sword; and I alone have escaped to tell
you." . . . Then Job arose, and rent his robe, and
shaved his head, and fell upon the ground, and
worshipped. And he said, *"Naked I came from my
mother's womb, and naked shall I return; Yahweh gave,
and Yahweh has taken away; blessed be the name of
Yahweh."* . . . And Yahweh blessed the latter days of
Job more than his beginning; and he had fourteen
thousand sheep, six thousand camels, a thousand
yoke of oxen, and a thousand she-asses. (Job 1:1, 3,
13a, 14–17, 20–21; 42:12)

Again the example is an artificial one. Job, an utterly
devout and extremely wealthy man from the eastern
country, who is directly reminiscent of the God-fearing
and wealthy Abraham, loses all his possessions through
a series of strokes of fate. In spite of this he holds on to
his trust in God, and because of that Yahweh makes up
for all he has lost. The didactic purpose is obvious: in
the end, an unshaken fear of God will be rewarded.

This story, too, has been expanded in a number
of different ways. The burning question whether it
is really God who plunges the devout into misfortune brings on to the scene a second, subordinate
author of the misfortune. Now it is *Satan* (Heb.: "the
adversary")—he is introduced as one of "the sons of
God," a figure belonging to the heavenly court—who
suggests putting Job's piety to the test. Since God is
sure of his follower, he consents. Thus the initiative

for Job's adversities no longer proceeds from God. The pattern has been influential, right down to Goethe's *Faust*. At the same time the misfortunes are multiplied, in order to intensify Job's piety still more. All his ten children are taken from him. A second series of disasters is made to follow the first. Covered with sores, Job sits in the ashes and scratches himself with a potsherd—the extreme of human misery. But at the same time he affirms what he has once said: "Shall we receive good at the hand of God, and shall we not receive evil?" (Job 2:10).

The pious example is much too simplistic to bridge the gulf between faith and experience. Consequently a *dialogue* has been inserted between Job's misfortune and his new felicity. It is this that has given the book its real stature, and has made it one of the great works of world literature. Three friends visit Job: Eliphaz the Temanite, Bildad the Shuhite, and Zophar the Naamathite. For seven days and seven nights they sit silently beside him in the ashes. Then Job breaks out: he curses the day when he was born (Job 3:1–26). The devout endurer becomes the rebel against God. The friends respond, one after the other, each of them in a long speech. They put forward the usual arguments propounded by theology. Each time Job gives an answer. The dialogue advances through three exchanges, and ends in a great indictment of God (Job 29–30):

> My prosperity has passed away like a cloud.
> And now my soul is poured out within me;
> days of affliction have taken hold of me. . . .
> I cry to you and you do not answer me;

I stand, and you do not heed me.
You have turned cruel to me;
with the might of your hand you persecute me.
You lift me up on the wind. . . .
and you toss me about in the roar of the storm.
Yes, I kn)w that you will bring me to death,
and to th ₂ house appointed for all the living.
(Job 30:15–23*)

At the end, using the form of the legal oath of purity which is also known to us from the 125th chapter of the Egyptian Book of the Dead (ANET 34–36; COS 2.12; AEL 2. 124–32), Job solemnly declares his innocence and complete devoutness, and challenges God to answer him (Job 31). He receives his answer. Originally it was probably as brief as what we now have in Job 40:1–5:

And Yahweh said to Job: "Shall a faultfinder contend with the Almighty? He who argues with God, let him answer it." Then Job answered Yahweh: "Behold, I am of small account; what shall I answer you? I lay my hand on my mouth. I have spoken once, and I will not answer; twice, but I will proceed no further."

The way Job in his misery rebels and then after a brief answer collapses and falls silent accentuates to the utmost the question about God's justice. Such a thorn in the flesh has incited theologians to ever new literary approaches and may have provoked the dialogue itself, which can hardly have started out as an independent poem, since it is a reaction to what takes place in the frame-story. And even in itself the dialogue is in no way a literary unity—which in no way detracts from its splendor.

The problem of Job is a general one. Everyone who has retained his faith in a higher justice can enter into it on the basis of his own experience. Even in the Ancient Near East a kind of Job literature was widespread. An early example is the Babylonian writing *ludlul bēl nēmeqi* ("I will praise the Lord of wisdom"; ANET 434–37, COS 1.153; BWL 21–56), which dates from the twelfth century BCE. But the qualitative leap is unmistakeable: the Jewish picture of God—faith in the almighty power of the good—gave the problem an intensity that was previously unknown.

RUTH

This touching tale appears today in the form of an idyll, but in fact it is the story of a pattern legal case. This case has to do with the levirate marriage (Lat.: *levir*, "brother-in-law"): a closely related person, a "redeemer," is in duty bound to secure the descendants of a relative who died childless by marrying his widow (Deut. 25:5–10). The first-born son of this union then continues the family of the deceased, which thus remains in possession of its land.

Again the model is drawn from the story of the patriarchs. Just as Isaac, with his wife, escapes to the country of the Philistines in order to evade a famine and lives there as a foreigner (Gen. 26), so Elimelech with his wife, Naomi, and his sons, Mahlon ("Sickness") and Chilion ("Consumption"), move to Moab. It was only afterwards that the event was set later, in the era of the Judges, so that, in a subsequently added genealogy (Ruth 4:18–22), Ruth's son can be declared David's grandfather. Elimelech dies in Moab. His two sons take Moabite wives, Orpah and Ruth. But soon Mahlon and Chilion succumb to the fate indicated by their names: they die. Naomi then returns to Bethlehem in Judah, together with her two daughters-in-law.

There she immediately sees to it that the levirate law is applied. She has chosen Boaz for the role of the "redeemer," an imposing hero. Cunningly, she thinks of a way of bringing about his marriage with Ruth, the widow of her elder son. When at night Boaz winnows corn in his barn, and sleeps away from home, Ruth is to "uncover his nakedness" and to lie down beside him. When Boaz wakes up, Ruth formally asks him for marriage: "Spread your skirt over your maidservant, for you are the redeemer" (Ruth 3:9). Boaz consents, but must first come to an agreement with another possible redeemer. This takes place on the following morning, in the gate, before the assembled citizens as witnesses. The other redeemer renounces his preferential claim, and Mahlon's land and his widow are passed over to Boaz. Ruth becomes pregnant and bears a son, and Naomi is called blessed by the women.

The story is a counterpart to the story about Tamar, to whom first Onan and later Judah refuse the levirate marriage (Gen. 38). Disguised as a harlot, Tamar seizes her rights through a trick. In the book of Ruth, too, a woman is the active protagonist: the widow, Naomi.

The name of the book shows that the chief roles later shifted. Today emphasis lies on Ruth's exemplary faithfulness. The contrast to Orpah, who turns home halfway, emphasizes that Ruth is prepared to follow her mother-in-law to the foreign country and, like Abraham, to leave her father's house and kindred behind (Ruth 2:11; cf. Gen. 12:1). The Moabite woman converts to Judaism, and is richly rewarded for so doing.

CHAPTER 17

ON THE FRINGE OF THE CANON

Common to the three books to be mentioned here is their departure from the bounds of "normal" Old Testament theology. They have widened the spectrum of the Old Testament, giving it important fresh nuances.

THE SONG OF SOLOMON (SONG OF SONGS)

This collection of about thirty poems was subsequently attributed to Solomon, and got into the canon for that reason. Judging by the language, which shows a strong Aramaic influence and even has one Greek borrowing, the book was not composed before the Hellenistic period.

Most of it consists of thoroughly erotic lyrics, although in antiquity we do not find the subjective element which is the mark of love in its modern guise. In the ancient world, the individual, embedded in the community, did not feel that his love was unique. That did not lessen the lover's desire; indeed the way in which it was given poetic expression was even thereby benefited.

The poems are artistic compositions. They use fixed genres and have elements of role poetry and travesty. They are put alternately into the mouth of the man and the woman. The inferior position of the woman which characterized public life did not apply to the personal encounter.

The interplay between attraction and playful withdrawal, passionate longing and flight is recreated in masterly fashion. The erotic images are frank but not in the least shameless, although they positively press for the consummation of love.

> O that you were like a brother to me,
> that nursed at my mother's breast!
> If I met you outside, I would kiss you,
> and none would despise me.
> I would lead you and bring you
> into the house of my mother,
> and into the chamber of her that conceived me.
> I would give you spiced wine to drink,
> the juice of my pomegranates.
> O that his left hand were under my head,
> and that his right hand embraced me!
> I adjure you, O daughters of Jerusalem,
> that you stir not up nor awaken love until it please.
> (Song of Sol. 8:1–4; cf. 2:1–7)

What we find in these love poems is certainly not the spontaneous outpouring of the heart. They could hardly have come into being without a specific *occasion* in the life of the community. A particular help in understanding them is a Syrian cycle of peasant wedding poetry, a role play which could still be seen as late as the nineteenth century at country weddings in Syria. During the week-long wedding celebrations the bridal pair counted as king and queen. They were enthroned on the threshing floor, while the wedding guests sang songs similar to those in the Song of Solomon.

The fact that such a text could be found in the Bible is both awkward and beneficial. Of course the eroticism was not accepted just as it stands, but was allegorized and applied to the relationship between Yahweh and Israel, or between Christ and the church, or Christ and the devout soul. But at the same time, the eroticism was preserved, and from it fervent piety drew its biblically legitimated grounding. The book made it possible to put into words the passion inherent in every true love for God. It was Johann Gottfried Herder who rediscovered that these are true love songs (*Salomos Lieder der Liebe*, 1778).

ECCLESIASTES, OR THE PREACHER

This writing is more of a philosophical tract than a religious book. With its sceptical turn of mind and its down-to-earth sobriety, it has always also appealed to readers who view religion with a degree of reserve. "The Song of Songs and Ecclesiastes," wrote Ernest Renan justly, "are like a love song and an essay of Voltaire's which have got lost between the folios of a theological library." But for all that, the basic impulse is eminently religious.

One reads the book like a collection of contemplations ("I have seen everything that is done under the sun") and reflections ("I said in my heart"). A planned outline can only be detected here and there. The ideas circle again and again round the same questions, and the reader soon comes upon particular key terms or concepts: *'āmāl* (Heb.: "toil"), *hæbæl* (Heb.: "vanity"), *yitrôn* (Heb.: "advantage"), *helæq* (Heb.: "portion"). As in older Wisdom literature, the questions are related to the connection between knowledge and success in life. But the horizon has fundamentally changed. Here the "I" is prominent, and it is an "I" who no longer views himself as part of the universal order, but tries to penetrate the world as something that is external and alien.

The wise man enquires about the "whole" of reality, that is to say, about God. He is concerned with "all that is done under heaven" (Eccles. 1:13). But his questions are always brought up short at what are merely aspects. He is forced to recognize that the question of meaning cannot be solved: "All is vanity (Heb.: *hæbæl*) and a striving after wind." The eternal cycles of nature and history are transient and of no avail. Their course has no purpose.

However, this conviction does not lead simply to a refusal to live but, on the contrary, to a resolute *carpe diem*—the determination to enjoy the day:

> A living dog is better than a dead lion. For the living know that they will die, but the dead know nothing, and they have no more reward; but the memory of them is lost. . . . So go, eat your bread with enjoyment, and drink your wine with a merry heart; for God has already approved what you do. Let your garments be always white; let not oil be lacking on your head. Enjoy life with the wife whom you love, . . . because that is your portion

[Heb.: *helæq*] in life and in your toil [Heb.: *'āmāl*] at
which you toil under the sun. (Eccles. 9:4–9*)

According to this doctrine about the allotted portion,
the art of living lies in contentment. By accepting the
limitation of what he knows of the world and God as
the lot God has assigned to him, and by renouncing
the question about the meaning of the whole, he gains
his limited success in life.

Even on this latest level of Old Testament Wisdom,
Solomon counts as the quintessence of the wise man.
But the book cannot go back to him, if only for the
reason that it is written in the latest form of biblical
Hebrew. Its world of ideas, too, is inconceivable in the
pre-Hellenistic era. The Hebrew name of the author,
Qohelet, which can just as well be a title, is a feminine
participle of the verb *qhl* (Heb.: "gather"). The English
name "Ecclesiastes" is taken from the title in the Greek
Bible, "Ekklesiastes," which corresponds to *ekklesia*
(Gk.: "assembly" ["church"]). From this came the alternative title "The Preacher." But these reflections are
suited neither to the marketplace nor to the pulpit.

ESTHER

The book begins like an oriental fairytale. Under King
Ahasuerus of Persia (i.e., Xerxes I, 486–465/64 BCE),
Queen Vashti fell into disgrace because she refused to
show her beauty openly on the occasion of a festal
banquet. In order to find a new queen, the great king
has all the beautiful virgins in the land brought to
him. He spends one night with each of them. Among

them there is also an orphan called Esther. She gains
the favor of the harem's overseer, Hegai, and with his
help wins the king's love. Ahasuerus makes her queen
(Esther 1:1–2, 18).

This tale is linked with a second tradition, which is
a farcical story illustrating the consequences of arro-
gance. The king elevates above all the other princes a
man called Haman, one of his courtiers. To Haman's
annoyance, the Jew Mordecai refuses to bow down to
him. In the evening the news items of the day are read
to the king. He learns that Mordecai has prevented a
murderous attack on him. The king asks Haman, who
is standing in the outer court: "What shall be done to
the man whom the king delights to honor?" Haman
supposes that he himself is meant, and suggests that a
prince should bring the man royal robes and a horse,
and should have him proclaimed the king's favorite.
Haman's punishment follows fast on the heels of his
conceit: he himself must publicly honor his antago-
nist, Mordecai (Esther 3:1–2, 5; 6:1–11).

These two models later became the basis for a narrative with which the Jewish community in the Diaspora
tried to master its fear of persecution. Out of anger
over Mordecai, Haman now proposes to the king that
he should order a general pogrom:

> There is a certain people scattered abroad and dis-
> persed among the peoples in all the provinces of
> your kingdom; their laws are different from those
> of every other people, and they do not keep the
> king's laws, so that it is not for the king's profit to
> tolerate them. (Esther 3:8)

The king ought to have them all killed on one and the same day, and their property, ten thousand talents of silver, should be paid into the state treasuries. Accepting this suggestion, the king elevates it into a law, which is proclaimed throughout the land. Even the non-Jewish population is dismayed.

Mordecai has the disastrous message brought to Queen Esther, who meanwhile counts as being his adopted daughter and niece. Esther summons up all her courage and, dangerous though it is, approaches the king, in order to invite him and Haman to a dinner. When the two appear, Esther informs the king of Haman's criminal plan. Haman ends on the gallows which he had prepared for Mordecai, and Mordecai is given Haman's position. He causes the king to issue a counteredict granting religious liberty to the Jews throughout the land, and giving them the right to resist their adversaries, many of whom are then killed.

By way of a later addition in 9:20–32, the story has been declared to be the legend behind the Purim festival, which is celebrated on the fourteenth and fifteenth days of the month Adar. In 3:7, Haman, after drawing lots (Heb.: *pûr*), decides on the thirteenth day of Adar as the day when the Jews are to be attacked. But the link is superficial. Underlying the Purim festival, which was originally only celebrated in the eastern Diaspora, there is probably a Babylonian or Persian New Year's festival, at which prospects for the coming year were ascertained through the drawing of lots (Heb.: *pûrîm*).

Judging by its language, the book dates from the later Hellenistic period. The Persian court is no more than an imaginative backcloth. Esther is the only biblical book of which no traces have been found in Qumran. The Septuagint offers two different versions, which are a kind of Greek midrash and which include narrative expansions. Whether the book should be included in the canon was disputed until the end (see page 173). More than two thousand years of Jewish persecution have allowed it to retain its topical force.

THE MACCABEAN PERIOD AND THE RISE OF APOCALYPTIC

The Book of Daniel

Daniel is the latest book in the Hebrew Old Testament, and it is the only thoroughgoing apocalypse to have found acceptance into the Bible of rabbinic Judaism. The apocalypse, as literary genre, was widespread in Judaism between the second century BCE and the first century CE, but ceased to be handed down after that. It is characterized by the expectation of a fundamental, world-shaking turn of events, whose arrival is predicted in cryptic revelations (visions), and whose date is calculated from the course of previous history. These writings were transmitted by devout groups which were suffering under severe oppression. Through the study of the prophets, and with the help of what they knew of history and astronomical-astrological data, they developed an arcane lore about the course of world events. They held the increasing oppression to be a sign that they were living in the final era of history, and hoped that through their obedience to the Torah they would escape when God came to inflict on sinners the punishment they deserved.

The story of the book of Daniel is set in the time of the Babylonian exile. But even the Neoplatonic philosopher Porphyry (232/33–304/5 CE) already maintained in his polemical work *Against the Christians* that the book is actually describing the oppression of the Jews by the Seleucid king Antiochus IV Epiphanes (175–164 BCE). Today this judgment is not in dispute, at least as far as the book's final version is concerned. The traditions were passed down by devout groups faithful to the Law, who were in dire straits as a result of Antiochus's religious policy. These groups were probably closely related to the Hasideans. Only the older sources of the book could be earlier than this period, but even they cannot possibly go back to the exile.

The book is made up of two parts, of differing provenance. Daniel 1–6 is an anthology of stories probably dating from the third century BCE, the early Hellenistic period. Each of its scenes can stand by itself. Daniel 7–12, on the other hand, presents a sequence of great visions, which have been added, step by step, to the book in the form in which it existed at the respective time. In Daniel 2:4 the language changes from Hebrew to Aramaic. The narrator makes King Nebuchadnezzar's soothsayers talk to the king in their own language. This change of language continues until the end of Daniel 7. It is only in Daniel 8–12 that the book reverts to Hebrew.

The stories about Daniel and his companions at the Babylonian court display both the religious pride of the Jewish Diaspora community and the oppression under which they suffered. Among these stories is the familiar and frequently painted theme of Daniel in the lions' den (Dan. 6). Daniel 5 has also become familiar to music-lovers through William Walton's powerful choral work *Belshazzar's Feast* (1931). The story accuses Belshazzar (*Bēl-šar(ra)-uṣur*), the last Babylonian governor in Babylon, of having misused at a banquet the Temple vessels stolen from Jerusalem. He pays for this with his life. During the wanton revels, a hand appears on the wall, and writes an inscription which no one but Daniel can interpret:

> This is the writing that was inscribed: MENE, MENE, TEKEL, and PARSIN. This is the interpretation of the matter: MENE, God has numbered the days of your kingdom and brought it to an end; TEKEL, you have been weighed in the balance and found wanting; PERES, your kingdom is divided and given to the Medes and the Persians. (Dan. 5:25–28)

The *mene tekel* (Hab.: "the writing on the wall") has become a familiar image, and the phrase "weighed in the balance and found wanting" has also become part of the language.

The cycle of the great apocalyptic visions in the second part of the book culminates in Daniel 12. Under the oppression of Antiochus, the writer sees history advancing inexorably towards the great crisis, after which everything will change.

> There shall be a time of trouble, such as never has been since there was a nation till that time; but at that time your people shall be delivered, every one whose name shall be found written in the book. And many of those who sleep in the dust of the earth

shall awake, some to everlasting life, and some to shame and everlasting contempt. (Dan. 12:1–2)

God's justice will be so all-embracing that even those who are already dead will rise from their graves, in order to be justified or, it may be, condemned. It is here that we find the roots of the idea of the Last Judgment, which so profoundly influenced mediaeval theology.

THE CLOSE OF THE CANON

In Jewish tradition the canonization of the Torah has become associated with the name of Ezra. In Nehemiah 8 we are told that Ezra read aloud publicly "the book of the Torah of Moses" in the square before the Water Gate. A closer look, however, shows that all that is said is that Ezra obeyed the command that the Torah should be proclaimed every seven years (Deut. 31:9–13). This cannot be seen as a formal canonization, all the less so since such an external act would have contradicted the inner nature of the canonization process. Moreover the event would have had to take place between the middle and the end of the fifth century BCE, when essential parts of the Torah were not yet in existence.

THE END OF THE GROWTH OF THE TEXT

Instead we can observe only that from the end of the Persian period the ongoing growth of the text gradually dried up. Beginning with the Torah, a fixed text crystallized out. A clue is offered by the fact that when the Samaritan Jews broke away from the Jerusalem community (probably towards the end of the fourth century BCE) it was only the Torah which they took over as their Holy Scripture. The former and latter prophets arrived at a comparable standing among the Jews in Jerusalem only later, although even then without achieving the rank of the Torah.

A possible reason for the fixing of the text was the increasing spread of the Jewish Diaspora in the Hellenistic world. At first, people resorted to correspondence with the priesthood in Jerusalem about doctrinal decisions, or even managed to have the Holy Scriptures sent from Jerusalem for them to look at. According to 2 Macc. 2:13–15, there had allegedly been a depository of sacred books in Jerusalem from the middle of the fifth century BCE. The writings collected there were unique copies, which are supposed to have been put at the disposal of the Egyptian Jews as a loan. But as soon as copies were made, it was important that the whole worldwide Jewish community should possess the same texts. Since in many cases the Septuagint (i.e., the Hebrew text behind its translation) represents the older reading, we can deduce that it was in the Diaspora that the text first hardened into a fixed form. But in Jerusalem, too, limits were now set to further revision.

THE SCOPE OF THE COLLECTION

Around 190 BCE, the so-called Praise of the Fathers in Sirach (Ecclesiasticus) 44–49 listed all the great figures in the Old Testament, from Enoch to Nehemiah.

Among them are Moses, David, and Solomon as writers, as well as Isaiah, Jeremiah, and Ezekiel. One remarkable sentence runs: "May the bones of the twelve prophets revive from where they lie, for they comforted the people of Jacob and delivered them with confident hope" (Sir 49:10). This shows that at this time the Book of the Twelve Prophets already existed as a collection, and with it the whole prophetic canon—which does not mean that the text could not still have been expanded later. The psalms ("David") and some of the Wisdom writings ("Solomon") were also already included in the canonical collection.

The oldest complete register of the Hebrew canon is provided by the Jewish writer Flavius Josephus, in his *Against Apion* (c. 95 CE). He lists 22 writings "which contain the records of all the past times; which are justly believed to be divine" (1.8). The number 22 corresponds to the number of letters in the Hebrew alphabet, and symbolizes the rounded-off completion of the collection. The more or less contemporary apocalyptic writing 4 Ezra lists 24 books (14:42–46). This has remained the Jewish numbering ever since. "The one who brings more than the 24 books into his house brings into his house confusion" (Midrash Qoheleth 12:12). This number, too, is symbolic: $24 = 2 \times 12$. It is arrived at because the books of Samuel, Kings, and Chronicles are not divided, and the books of Ezra and Nehemiah, as well as the Book of the Twelve Prophets, are seen as single units. In addition Josephus has probably assigned Ruth to Judges, and Lamentations to Jeremiah.

CRITERIA FOR CANONICITY

Josephus also names a criterion for defining the revelatory character of the collection:

> With us it is not open to everybody to write the
> records, and there is no discrepancy in what is writ-
> ten; on the contrary, the prophets alone had this
> privilege, obtaining their knowledge of the most re-
> mote and ancient history through the inspiration
> which they owed to God, and committing to writ-
> ing a clear account of the events of their own time
> just as they occurred. (*Against Apion,* 1.7)

In short, the criterion is prophecy. This had a tremendous influence, from the doctrine of inspiration
held in Christian dogmatics, down to nineteenth-
century idealistic exegesis, and it has been one of the
greatest hindrances to the historical criticism of the
Bible.

Even Josephus, who was bound to the criterion of
prophecy, was forced to interpret because of it. The
traditional biblical writers, one and all, are declared to
be prophets, even Moses, David, and Solomon. In the
Talmud, the individual writings are then assigned precisely to their supposed prophetic authors (Tractate
Baba bathra 14b–15a). But as far as the canon of the
Holy Scriptures is concerned, the inescapable consequence is that prophecy is bound to come to an end
with the close of the canon: Ezra, the last author in the
biblical canon, was the last of the prophets. From this
time on there is no more prophecy, only interpretation.
The flood of deutero-canonical literature, however,

shows that this principle was not rigidly applied. One way of getting round it was the pseudepigraphy.

THE FINAL ESTABLISHMENT OF THE CANON

Josephus presupposes that the fixed Jewish canon already exists. The final decisions which were required had just been made, at the end of the first century CE. Just as from this time on rabbinic exegesis was related to a single textual form—the proto-Masoretic text—it also required a firmly defined body of writings.

The greater part of the collection had crystallized long before, and was a matter of course. The debates as to which books "the hands sully" (i.e., which books are holy) are recorded in the Mishnah, Tractate Yadaim ("Hands") 3.5. In the end, the only books which were in doubt were the Song of Solomon, Ecclesiastes, and Esther (cf. Bab.Talmud, Tractate Megillah 7a), all for understandable reasons. The Song of Solomon and Ecclesiastes were accepted because they were held to have been written by Solomon. Esther was included because the fictitious happenings take place before Ezra. These debates probably took place in Jamnia, on the Palestine coastal plain, which between 70 and 135 CE was the seat of the Great Sanhedrin. It has been assumed that a synod was held there, but there is no mention of this in the sources.

※

THE OLD TESTAMENT: AN OPEN BOOK

The literary process from which the Old Testament emerged has never really come to a stop: "Of making many books there is no end" (Eccles. 12:12). An end would be incompatible with the nature of a text which continually presses for fresh interpretation—interpretation not only of the text itself, but interpretation of the world through the text.

Consequently the Old Testament has left its traces throughout the whole of history. The deutero-canonical literature, as well as the Qumran writings and the New Testament, are its legacy. Rabbinic exegesis made the Old Testament its object, as did the Bible commentaries of the church fathers. The Koran, too, indirectly belongs within the orbit of the Bible's influence. From the end of the fourteenth century CE, the Bible increasingly became the yardstick against which criticism of the church was measured, and from the sixteenth-century Reformation, with the resulting translations into the European vernaculars, it again became in a vital way the basis of Christianity, which, in the churches of the Reformation, acquired the character of a scriptural faith. With the beginning of general education, the Bible became the school book *par excellence*. It was the Bible which molded the picture of the world and the human being.

For long stretches the history of European art is an interpretation of the Bible in building, sculpture, and painting. Its influence on literature is immeasurable. European music grew out of the setting of the psalms. If knowledge of the Bible disappears, as it threatens to do in the modern world, the cultural and religious loss will be irreplaceable.

Last but not least, historical criticism belongs within the orbit of the Bible itself. Especially from the European Enlightenment onwards, exegesis learnt step by step to read the Bible as a historically conditioned source. It began to be seen as a document from the ancient world which was not created in order to provide doctrinal tenets for the dogmatists. Scholars discovered, and are continually discovering afresh, the difference between the biblical account of history and history as it actually took place. Israelite-Jewish antiquity is emerging before our eyes with an undreamt-of vitality. The Bible is acquiring a new profile.

This also means subjecting the influence of the Bible to ideological criticism, with the help of the Bible itself. Scholarly exegesis has the task of protecting Jewish and Christian faith from the religious fundamentalism which appeals to the Bible as if it were a paper fetish. Right down to the present day, the Bible has been misused for the purposes of self-defense, and to underpin religious and even political claims, as if it came down from heaven. But the Bible is not an absolute book; it is a historical one. If it reveals the absolute, the absolute is veiled in the relative. Consequently the Bible resists any one-sided claim, but is open for many, even rival interpretations. The dispute about the Old Testament cannot come to an end, and must never be allowed to do so.

The impossibility of grasping fully the message which in the end announces nothing less than the new heaven and the new earth, is shown at the very point where we read: "Today this scripture has been fulfilled in your hearing"(Luke 4:21). For what the Christian faith has interpreted as fulfilment was, for ears and eyes, failure: the death of Jesus of Nazareth on the cross. But it was precisely here that for Christians the Jewish inheritance retained its validity—not as proof of their own claim to the "correct" interpretation, but as God's enduring promise.

All this being so, what we hold in our hands is not merely one of the most impressive documents in the whole history of religion. It is the testimony of a faith which has been able to inspire men and women right through the centuries, down to the present day: *Tolle lege*—"Pick it up and read it!"

Appendix A

The Books of the Old Testament

Genesis	Gen.	(*bᵉreʾšît*, 1st Book of Moses)
Exodus	Exod.	(*šᵉmôt*, 2nd Book of Moses)
Leviticus	Lev.	(*wayyiqrāʾ*, 3rd Book of Moses)
Numbers	Num.	(*bᵉmidbār*, 4th Book of Moses)
Deuteronomy	Deut.	(*dᵉbārîm*, 5th Book of Moses)
Joshua	Josh.	
Judges	Judg.	(*šôpᵉṭîm*, Judices)
Ruth		
1 Samuel	1 Sam.	
2 Samuel	2 Sam.	
1 Kings		(*mᵉlākîm*, Reges)
2 Kings		
1 Chronicles	1 Chron.	(*dibrê hayyāmîm*, Paralipomena, Verba dierum)
2 Chronicles	2 Chron.	
Ezra		
Nehemiah	Neh.	
Tobit	Tob.	
Judith	Jdt.	
Esther	Esth.	
1 Maccabees	1 Macc.	
2 Maccabees	2 Macc.	

Job		
Psalms	Ps.	(*t^{e}hillîm*)
Proverbs	Prov.	(*mišlê*, Proverbia)
Ecclesiastes (The Preacher)	Eccles.	
Song of Solomon (Song of Songs)	Song of Sol.	(*šîr haššîrîm*, Canticum canticorum)
Wisdom	Wisd.	(Sapientia Salomonis)
Sirach	Sir.	(Ecclesiasticus)
Isaiah	Isa.	
Jeremiah	Jer.	
Lamentations	Lam.	(*'êkāh*, Threni)
Baruch	Bar.	
Epistle of Jeremiah (= Bar. 6)	EpJer	
Ezekiel	Ezek.	
Daniel	Dan.	
Hosea	Hos.	
Joel		
Amos		
Obadiah	Obad.	
Jonah	Jon.	
Micah	Mic.	
Nahum	Nah.	
Habakkuk	Hab.	
Zephaniah	Zeph.	
Haggai	Hag.	
Zechariah	Zech.	
Malachi	Mal.	

Appendix B

The Hebrew Bible

The Torah

- Genesis
- Exodus
- Leviticus
- Numbers
- Deuteronomy

The Former Prophets

- Joshua
- Judges
- Samuel
- Kings

The Latter Prophets

- Isaiah
- Jeremiah
- Ezekiel
- The Book of the Twelve Prophets
  - Hosea
  - Joel
  - Amos
  - Obadiah
  - Jonah
  - Micah
  - Nahum
  - Habakkuk
  - Zephaniah
  - Haggai
  - Zechariah
  - Malachi

The Writings

- Psalms
- Job
- Proverbs
- The Scrolls
  - Ruth
  - Song of Songs
  - Ecclesiastes
  - Lamentations
  - Esther
- Daniel
- Ezra and Nehemiah
- Chronicles

Appendix C

The Septuagint

The Five Books of Moses

Genesis
Exodus
Leviticus
Numbers
Deuteronomy

The Historical Books

Joshua
Judges
Ruth
1 Kings (=1 Sam.)
2 Kings (=2 Sam.)
3 Kings (=1 Kings)
4 Kings (=2 Kings)
1 Chronicles
2 Chronicles
(3 Ezra)
Ezra and Nehemiah
Esther (with additions)
Judith
Tobit
1 Maccabees
2 Maccabees
(3 Maccabees)
(4 Maccabees)

The Didactic Books

Psalms (with Odes)
Proverbs
Ecclesiastes
Song of Solomon
Job
Wisdom
Sirach
(Psalms of Solomon)

The Prophetic Books

Hosea
Amos
Micah
Joel
Obadiah
Jonah
Nahum
Habakkuk
Zephaniah
Haggai
Zechariah
Malachi
Isaiah
Jeremiah
Baruch
Lamentations
Epistle of Jeremiah
Ezekiel
Daniel (with additions)

CHRONOLOGICAL OUTLINE

1224–1204 BCE	Pharaoh Merenptah. In an inscription of this Pharaoh's, *Israel* is mentioned for the first time.
c.1200	The empires of the late Bronze Age collapse.
c.1000	Emergence of the kingdoms of Israel and Judah and their neighbors. Kings Abimelech, Saul, David, Solomon.
926	Separation of the kingdom of Israel and Judah.
882–871	King Omri, the founder of the Northern Kingdom's most important dynasty. Israel emerges into the light of history.
871–852	King Ahab ben Omri. The prophet Elijah. The god *Yahweh* becomes the god of the Omride dynasty, as also of the Davidic dynasty, to which the Omrides were related by marriage.
845	Jehu overthrows the Omride dynasty; his dynasty rules until 747.
745–727	Tiglath-Pileser III; Assyria becomes a major power.
736	King Uzziah (Asariah) of Judah dies. Call of the prophet Isaiah.
734 or 733	Aram and Israel attack Judah (Syrian-Ephraimitic War). The prophets Hosea and Amos.
733	Judah becomes an Assyrian vassal state.
727–722	Shalmaneser V of Assyria; he conquers the Northern Kingdom, Israel, and besieges Samaria.

722	Sargon II of Assyria conquers Samaria. Israel becomes the Assyrian province of Samerina.
701	Sennacherib of Assyria conquers Judah. Jerusalem under Hesekiah is spared.
Mid-7th century	Gradual decline of the Assyrian empire.
639–609	King Josiah. Judah's last golden age. Josiah concentrates the official Yahweh cult in Jerusalem. The Deuteronomic Law.
612	Medes and Neo-Babylonians conquer Nineveh. The end of Assyria.
609	Josiah is killed at Megiddo by Pharaoh Neco II. Palestine comes under Egyptian sovereignty. The prophet Jeremiah begins his proclamation.
605	Nebuchadnezzar II of Babylonia defeats the Egyptians at Carchemish. Palestine comes under Neo-Babylonian sovereignty.
597	Nebuchadnezzar conquers Jerusalem for the first time. King Jehoiachin is deported to Babylon. The beginning of the Jewish Diaspora. The Yahwist's History is conceived.
586	Nebuchadnezzar conquers Jerusalem for the second time and has the Temple, palace and city walls destroyed; the rule of the kings belonging to the house of David breaks off.
562–560	Amel-marduk of Babylonia; under him Jehoiachin is rehabilitated.
556–539	Nabonidus of Babylonia. Decline of Neo-Babylonian power. Hopes for the restoration of the Davidic kingship. The Deuteronomistic History is conceived.
539	Cyrus II of Persia conquers Babylon.

525	Cambyses of Persia conquers Egypt. Palestine falls to the Persians.
520–515	Judah is incorporated into the Persian provincial system under Darius I. The Temple in Jerusalem is rebuilt. The Jewish community takes form.
445/44	Nehemiah in Jerusalem. Rebuilding of the city walls.
332	Alexander the Great in Palestine. Beginning of the Hellenistic era.
301	Battle of Ipsos. Palestine falls to the Ptolemies.
285–246	Ptolemy II Philadelphos; under him, according to legend, the Torah is translated into Greek. Beginning of the Greek Old Testament (the Septuagint).
(200) 198	Battle of Paneas; Palestine falls to the Seleucids.
169–167	Antiochus IV Epiphanes attacks the Temple in Jerusalem.
166–164	Maccabean uprising. The book of Daniel is conceived, this being the latest book in the Hebrew Old Testament.
After 132	The prologue to the Greek book of Sirach probably presupposes that the translation of the Old Testament into Greek has been completed.
129–163	The Hasmonean monarchy.
2nd century BCE	First Isaiah scroll, later found in Cave 1 in Qumran.
63 BCE	Pompey conquers Jerusalem.
37 BCE–44 CE	The Herodian monarchy.

66–74 CE	First Jewish uprising. At this time the Qumran manuscripts were hidden in the caves near the Dead Sea.
70	Destruction of Jerusalem.
End of 1st century	Final decisions about the scope of the Hebrew canon. The (proto-)Masoretic text becomes the authoritative text form in Judaism.
132–135	Second Jewish uprising.
c.230–240	Origen's recension of the Septuagint (the *Hexapla*).
4th century	Codex Vaticanus, the oldest complete manuscript of the Greek Old Testament.
c.390–405	Jerome translates the Hebrew text into Latin (the Vulgate).
6th–8th century	Manuscripts from the Cairo Genizah.
8th–10th century	Two families of scholars, ben Asher and ben Naftali, in Tiberias on Lake Gennesaret vocalize the Masoretic text.
1008	Codex Petropolitanus (= Codex Lenigradensis), the oldest complete manuscript of the Hebrew Old Testament.

FURTHER READING

Literary History

Barton, J. and J. Muddiman, *Oxford Bible Commentary*, Oxford and New York, 2001.

Blenkinsopp, J., *The Pentateuch: An introduction to the first five books of the Bible*, New York, 1992.

Friedman, R. E., *Who wrote the Bible?* San Francisco, 1997 (popular; also in the framework of generally accepted theories).

Kaiser, O., *Introduction to the Old Testament: A presentation of its results and problems*, trans. J. Sturdy, Oxford and Minneapolis, 1975 (account of the present state of research).

Schmidt, W. H., *Old Testament Introduction*, trans. M. J. O'Connell, New York and Louisville, 1999 (for the general reader, remains in the framework of generally accepted theories).

Smend, R., *Die Entstehung des Alten Testaments*, 4th ed., Stuttgart, 1989 (important standard textbook, starting from the final stage of the Old Testament).

VanderKam, J. C., *The Dead Sea Scrolls Today*, Grand Rapids and London, 1994.

History of the Biblical Text

Tov, E., *Textual Criticism of the Hebrew Bible*, 2d ed., Minneapolis and Assen, 2001 (up to date and comprehensive).

Würthwein, E., *The Text of the Old Testament: An introduction to the Biblia Hebraica*, trans. E. F. Rhodes, 2d ed., Grand Rapids, 1995 (well illustrated).

Methodology

Barton, J., *Reading the Old Testament: Method in biblical study*, 2d ed., London, 1996.

Fishbane, M. A., *Biblical Interpretation in Ancient Israel*, Oxford and New York, 1985 (introduction to the inner-biblical interpretation process).

Historiography

Noth, M., *The Deuteronomistic History*, trans. J. Dossall et al., Sheffield, 1981.

————., *The Chronicler's History*, translated and with an introduction by H.G.M. Williamson, Sheffield, 1987.

Van Seters, J., *In Search of History: Historiography in the ancient world and the origins of biblical history*, New Haven and London, 1983.

Wellhausen, J., *Prolegomena to the History of Israel*, trans. J. Sutherland Black and A. Menzies, with preface by W. Robertson Smith, Edinburgh 1885; reprint, Atlanta, 1994 (fundamental for the historical understanding of the Old Testament).

Psalms

Seybold, K., *Introducing the Psalms*, trans. R. Graeme Dunphy, Edinburgh, 1990 (short outline of all of the important viewpoints of psalm exegesis).

Wisdom Literature

Collins J. J., *Jewish Wisdom in the Hellenistic Age*, Louisville and Edinburgh, 1997.

Crenshaw, J. L., *Old Testament Wisdom: an introduction*, Louisville, 1998.

von Rad, G., *Wisdom in Israel*, trans. J. D. Martin, Nashville and London, 1972 (a famous account).

History of Israel

Finkelstein, I. and N. A. Silberman, *The Bible Unearthed: Archaeology's new vision of ancient Israel and the origin of its sacred texts*, New York, London, Toronto, Sydney, and Singapore, 2001.

Grabbe, L. L., *Judaism from Cyrus to Hadrian*, Minneapolis, 1992.

Miller, J. M. and J. H. Hayes, *A History of Ancient Israel and Judah*, London, 1999.

VanderKam, J. C., *An Introduction to Early Judaism*, Grand Rapids, 2001.

History of Religion

del Olmo Lete, G., *Canaanite Religion: According to the liturgical texts of Ugarit*, trans. W.G.E. Watson, Bethesda, Md., 1999.

Keel, O. and C. Uehlinger, *Gods, Goddesses, and Images of God in Ancient Israel*, trans. T. H. Trapp, Minneapolis, 1998 (important new approach).

van der Toorn, K., B. Becking, and P. W. van der Horst, eds., *Dictionary of Deities and Demons in the Bible*, 2d ed., Leyden, 1999 (DDD).

Theology of the Old Testament

Barr, J., *The Concept of Biblical Theology: An Old Testament perspective*, London and Minneapolis, 1999.

Childs, B. S., *Biblical Theology of the Old and New Testaments: Theological reflection on the Christian Bible*, Minneapolis, 1993.

von Rad, G., *Old Testament Theology*, trans. D.M.G. Stalker, I: *The theology of Israel's historical traditions*; II: *The theology of Israel's prophetic traditions*, Edinburgh and New York, 1962–65 (classic account).

Anthologies of Ancient Near Eastern Texts in English Translation

Davies, G. I., *Ancient Hebrew Inscriptions. Corpus and Concordance*, Cambridge, 1991 (AHI: Hebrew and English).

Hallo, W. W. and K. L. Younger, eds., *The Context of Scripture: Canonical compositions, monumental inscriptions, and archival documents from the biblical world*, Leyden, 1997–2002 (COS) (newest comprehensive collection).

Kaiser, O., ed., *Texte aus der Umwelt des Alten Testaments*, Gütersloh, 1982–2001 (TUAT) (comprehensive collection in German).

Lambert, W. G., *Babylonian Wisdom Literature*, Oxford, 1960; reprint Winona Lake, 1996 (BWL).

Lichtheim, M., *Ancient Egyptian Literature: A book of readings*, 3 vols., Berkeley, Los Angeles, and London, 1973–1980 (AEL) (study collection of Egyptian texts).

Pritchard, J. B., ed., *Ancient Near Eastern Texts Relating to the Old Testament*, 3d ed., Princeton, 1969 (ANET) (still valid).

Writings from the Ancient World, Atlanta: Society of Biblical Literature, 1990ff.

Intertestamental Literature

Charlesworth, J. H., *The Old Testament Pseudepigrapha*, New York, 1984–1985.

García Martínez, F. and E.J.C. Tigchelaar, *The Dead Sea Scrolls Study Edition*, Leyden, Boston, and Grand Rapids, 2000 (with English translation).

Dictionary to the Bible

Freedman, D. N., ed., *The Anchor Bible Dictionary*, 5 vols., New York, 1992 (ABD).

Historical Geography

Aharoni, Y., *The Land of the Bible: A Historical Geography*, Philadelphia, 1979 (comprehensive).

Rogerson, J. W., *The New Atlas of the Bible*, London, 1985 (popular).

Archaeology

Fritz, V., *An Introduction to Biblical Archaeology*, Eng. trans., Sheffield, 1994.

Mazar, A., *Archaeology of the Land of the Bible*, vol. 1: 10,000–586 BCE, New York, 1992; vol. 2: *The Assyrian, Babylonian and Persian Periods 732–332 BCE*, New York, 2001.

Myers, E. M., ed., *The Oxford Encyclopaedia of Archaeology in the Near East*, 5 vols., New York, 1997.

Stern, E., ed., *The New Encyclopaedia of Archaeological Excavations in the Holy Land*, Jerusalem, 1993.

Historical Atlases

Aharoni, Y. and M. Avi-Yonah, *The Carta Bible Atlas*, 4th ed., Jerusalem, 2002 (outline of biblical history in maps).

May, H. G., *Oxford Bible Atlas*, rev. 3d ed. by J. May, Oxford, 1984 (good maps).

Mittmann, S., ed., *Tübingen Bible Atlas*, Stuttgart, 2001 (selection from the famous *Tübingen Atlas des Vorderen Orients*).

Pritchard J. B., ed., *The Times Atlas of the Bible*, London, 1987 (= *The Harper Atlas of the Bible*, 3d ed., New York, 1994) (comprehensive visual material on the Bible).